Countdown to Creative Writing

This guide provides all the support you need in helping pupils to improve their prose writing. *Countdown to Creative Writing* is a comprehensive and flexible resource that you can use in different ways:

► Stand-alone modules that cover all the essential aspects of writing a story;

► Photocopiable activity sheets for each module that show how to make the decisions and solve the problems that all writers face along the road from first idea to finished piece of work;

► Teachers' notes with tips and guidance including how modules could be used as stand-alone units, but also with suggestions for useful links between modules, and curriculum links;

► A self-study component so that children can make their own progress through the materials, giving young writers a sense of independence in thinking about their work;

► Countdown flowcharts providing an overview showing how modules are linked and how teachers can progress through them with the children;

► 'Headers' for each module showing where along the 'countdown path' you are at that point.

In short *Countdown to Creative Writing* saves valuable planning time and gives you all the flexibility you need – teachers might want to utilise either the self-study or 'countdown' aspects of the book, or simply dip into it for individual lesson activities to fit in with their own programmes of work.

A former teacher, **Steve Bowkett** is now a full-time writer, storyteller, educational consultant and hypnotherapist. He is the author of more than forty books, including *Jumpstart! Creativity* and *Imagine That*.

Developing pupils' writing abilities boosts their confidence, creates enjoyment and relevance in the task and cultivates a range of decision-making and problem-solving skills that can then be applied across the curriculum. The Countdown series provides all the support you need in helping pupils to improve their prose, poetry and non-fiction writing.

Forthcoming titles in the series

Countdown to Poetry Writing
Steve Bowkett
978–0–415–47752–9

Countdown to Creative Writing

Step by step approach to writing techniques for 7–12 years

Steve Bowkett

Routledge
Taylor & Francis Group

LONDON AND NEW YORK

First published 2009
by Routledge
2 Park Square, Milton Park, Abingdon, Oxon OX14 4RN

Simultaneously published in the USA and Canada
by Routledge
711 Third Avenue, New York, NY 10017

Routledge is an imprint of the Taylor & Francis Group, an informa business

© 2009 Steve Bowkett

Typeset in Frutiger and Sassoon Primary by
Florence Production Ltd, Stoodleigh, Devon

British Library Cataloguing in Publication Data
A catalogue record for this book is available from the British Library

Library of Congress Cataloging in Publication Data
Bowkett, Steve.
    Countdown to creative writing: step by step approach to writing
techniques for 7–12 years/Steve Bowkett.
        p. cm.
    1. English language–Composition and exercises–Study and teaching
(Elementary) 2. Creative writing (Elementary education) I. Title.
    LB1576.B536 2008
    372.62'3044–dc22   2008018740

ISBN10: 0–415–46855–8 (pbk)
ISBN13: 978–0–415–46855–8 (pbk)

Contents

Overview – How to use the book

This book has been designed as a practical resource to help upper KS2 and lower KS3 pupils master the complex network of skills that contribute to what is commonly called 'creative writing', with the emphasis on prose fiction. The modules lead pupils through the process from how to generate first ideas to a polished draft piece of work and beyond.

The modules can be used as stand-alone units that the teacher may use within existing programmes of work, or be combined to form short topics on different aspects of creative writing – genre, characters, settings and so on. However, the activities are arranged such that pupils can also learn more independently by making their own decisions about what they need to know and therefore how to proceed from unit to unit. This 'choose your own adventure' format means that more confident and/or experienced writers can bypass modules that are not relevant or that would simply duplicate thinking they have already done. On the other hand, less experienced writers will benefit from the more highly scaffolded process of exploring the elements of writing at a more basic level, or in greater detail as appropriate.

Teacher's notes support most of the modules and offer tips on how you may best advise a pupil who feels stuck at any point. The notes also give suggestions on ways in which the activities can be extended and linked. A creative thinking approach to developing writing is encouraged throughout. As such the teacher's notes explain the 'thinking skills agenda' that underpins the modules and highlights the fact that as pupils become more effective thinkers in the context of writing, so those skills are transferred to other areas of the curriculum. In this regard creative writing is seen not just as one aspect of English or literacy, but as a vehicle for developing pupils' ability to 'learn how to learn' across the school subject range.

Teachers can plan their use of the modules, and pupils can track their own progress, by referring to the flowchart on page 4. This places a pupil's current task within the context of the broader writing process. Most of the activities are photocopiable, but to increase the usefulness of the resource some extra material is also accessible online at www.routledge.com/professional/9780415468558. Thus a teacher or pupil can click on a link to download and if required print off a copy of any activity. This helps to personalise the learning and will save the teacher the time and trouble of extensive photocopying as pupils can be accessing many different activities simultaneously.

An added benefit of the flowchart is that it acts as a visual organiser of the route an author takes in thinking through a project, so that pupils gain an overview of what is involved in writing a story as well as exploring specific threads of that greater tapestry.

The thinking skills agenda

Writing and thinking feed each other. Every writer's challenge is to *reach for the words* that express the thoughts going on inside his or her head. Teaching the craft of writing is most powerful when pupils are also taught to think more effectively. By the same token, thinking skills themselves can be developed by teaching writing.

In many books on thinking the distinction is made between creative and critical thinking skills. Basically creative thinking is defined as 'imaginative' thinking leading to new ideas through a synthesis of thoughts, while critical thinking is more analytical and looks for the reasoning behind structures of thought. Practically speaking, the act of writing uses both creative and critical thinking continuously. This is not the same thing as a pupil trying to analyse or otherwise judge and evaluate ideas and words as they emerge. One of the great inhibitors to fluent writing (i.e. an organic flow of ideas) is trying to edit sentences while they are being constructed. This is especially true during the earlier stages as ideas are being first formed and linked. In other words, if a pupil is trying to express an idea but is also worrying about where to place an apostrophe, the act of expression is likely to be stunted. Neatness and accuracy are important for clarity of course, but good practice in teaching writing does not insist on pupils trying to do everything at once.

Countdown to Creative Writing explains the thinking processes that build towards polished pieces of writing. It explores one methodology among many that are possible. As Somerset Maugham advised, there are three golden rules to good writing – and nobody knows what they are. A strategy that works well for one writer might leave another author cold. Having said that, the book assumes that more basic decisions such as whether a story will be Science Fiction or Romance, humorous or serious, are likely to be made early on in a pupil's thinking about the work. If that is not the case – for instance if a pupil has a great idea for a character first – then those ideas can be developed at the outset before other decisions are made. The modules in this book give advice and offer practical techniques on many aspects of writing. In using the units flexibly you will be modelling an important feature of the creative process – that if one tool isn't doing the job then look for or invent another tool that will.

Getting started

How to use the flowchart

The flowchart on page 4 gives an overview of the thinking a pupil might do in preparation for a first draft piece of writing. The boxes in **bold** show the basic steps to be taken, with different activities attached to support the decisions that need to be made and the techniques that need to be mastered. The modules can be used singly or in combination (decided upon by the teacher and/or the pupil). It is not likely that many pupils will want or need to look at all the modules. It's also important to realise that while the flowchart leads towards a first draft, that is not the only outcome; lots of writing will take place as pupils tackle the different modules.

Useful classroom tips

In guiding pupils in the use of the modules, you might find these basic points useful:

▶ The competitive ethos usually inhibits creative flow. If a pupil is concerned about whether his work is as good as his neighbour's, he is less likely to produce his best writing or enjoy the process as much. In other words, intending to do one's best is not the same as trying to be better than other people.

▶ A positive and supportive approach works better than a critical and corrective one. A well-known and effective strategy is called *3PPI* – offer three points of praise then one insight for improvement. Psychologically when a teacher notices three good things about a pupil's work he is more readily convinced that he's done well, and is then 'cushioned' to accept the suggestion for an area where improvement is needed.

▶ Modelling the attitude that you want to cultivate in the pupils works wonders. If they see you tackling some of the modules and having fun writing, they are more likely to do so too. Also by working through the modules yourself you experience the same problems, excitements and achievements as the pupils. You are then more than a writer – you become an author (see Review section).

▶ In supporting pupils' writing, bear in mind the Triangle of failure (Figure 1). Often what seems to be a failure of capability is actually a failure of imagination

Module
60

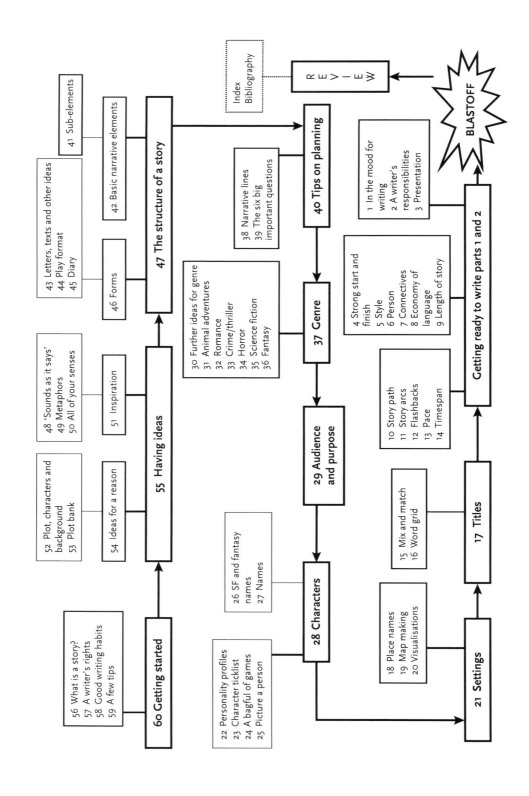

47 The structure of a story

41 Sub-elements

42 Basic narrative elements

43 Letters, texts and other ideas
44 Play format
45 Diary

46 Forms

Index
Bibliography

R
E
V
I
E
W

BLASTOFF

40 Tips on planning

38 Narrative lines
39 The six big important questions

1 In the mood for writing
2 A writer's responsibilities
3 Presentation

Getting ready to write parts 1 and 2

37 Genre

30 Further ideas for genre
31 Animal adventures
32 Romance
33 Crime/thriller
34 Horror
35 Science fiction
36 Fantasy

4 Strong start and finish
5 Style
6 Person
7 Connectives
8 Economy of language
9 Length of story

55 Having ideas

48 'Sounds as it says'
49 Metaphors
50 All of your senses

51 Inspiration

52 Plot, characters and background
53 Plot bank

54 Ideas for a reason

29 Audience and purpose

10 Story path
11 Story arcs
12 Flashbacks
13 Pace
14 Timespan

17 Titles

15 Mix and match
16 Word grid

28 Characters

26 SF and fantasy names
27 Names

22 Personality profiles
23 Character ticklist
24 A bagful of games
25 Picture a person

60 Getting started

56 What is a story?
57 A writer's rights
58 Good writing habits
59 A few tips

18 Place names
19 Map making
20 Visualisations

21 Settings

Module 60

and/or a failure of nerve. A failure of imagination means that a pupil is stuck in a *can't state* – 'I can't think of an idea, I can't imagine what my character looks like, I can't think of what to say next. Help I'm stuck!' A failure of nerve is a *daren't state*. The pupil does not dare to have a go through fear of doing it wrong or not being as good as someone else. When these issues are addressed (and this book will show you how), then pupils usually feel more capable and the triangle becomes one of success; supportive and synergistic.

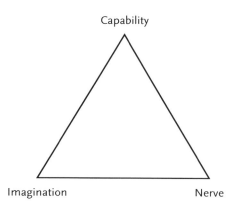

Figure 1 Triangle of failure

Module 60

Getting started

Hello

If you are reading this then you are about to go on an adventure. Just about every writer I know embarks on this adventure when he or she wants to do some writing. It is a thinking journey where you will be encouraged to play with ideas. By the way, I hope you like playing as much as I do!

Travelling with the flowchart

Look at the story flowchart. You'll see a route in **bold**. This is the path you might take on your voyage of the imagination. Perhaps you'll explore the whole path or, with your teacher's advice, just bits of it. When you travel, bear these points in mind.

Useful tips

▶ To have really good ideas it's best to have lots of ideas.

▶ No idea is ever wasted – so don't throw any away! Even ideas that don't seem to work might be very useful in the end.

▶ Every word you write is a step in the right direction. Even stuff you change or cross out is helping you to learn how to be a better author.

Now it might be that your teacher is deciding which modules you look at and in which order, but the modules are also designed for you to work more independently, with your teacher's support. If that's how you're doing it, you have a decision to make.

Take it further

▶ If you want a few basic tips about writing, go to **A few tips** (**Module 59**).

▶ If you want to learn about good writing habits, jump to **Good writing habits** (**Module 58**).

▶ If you would like to know about your basic 'writer's rights', leap to **A writer's rights** (**Module 57**).

▶ If you want an overview (a general picture) of the form your writing will take, go to **What is a story?** (**Module 56**).

▶ If you definitely want to write a story but haven't got an idea yet, jump to **Having ideas** (**Module 55**).

▶ If you have an idea for a story – go and speak with your teacher, who will suggest what you can do next.

A few tips

The essence of creative thinking

The essence of creative thinking is *being unafraid of ideas*. This is why the ethos of playfulness-in-exploration is so important. If a pupil is in a playful mood then she is more likely to become immersed in ideas and words to see how they work and what they can do. Wonderment (a state) leads to wondering (a process): natural curiosity focuses itself into ways of thinking and questioning, i.e. the very thinking skills we are cultivating, that at their highest level express themselves in an artful dance of synthesis and analysis; a 'spiral dynamic' of discovery at increasingly sophisticated levels.

Pupils are naturally filled with wonder. The world is wonder-full to them. Questioning is a completely normal process that illustrates two vital aspects of creative thinking:

▶ Mentally linking ideas that were previously separate and unrelated.

▶ Looking at things from different perspectives.

Both of these are features of our basic urge to *contextualise*. We are all 'nosy' – we have to know more. The root of the word context is 'to braid'. We naturally weave separate threads of knowing together as we make sense of the world. Contextualising turns knowledge into information – it is 'in-formation', an active forming of greater understanding. Context and 'text' are also etymologically connected. Any text is a tapestry of ideas, a weaving-up of meanings to form a more complex structure.

Encouraging pupils in their thinking

When we encourage pupils in their thinking and writing we are giving them the courage to be playful in the face of increasing creative and intellectual demands. To encourage means 'to give courage to'. As teachers we do that most effectively by being unafraid of ideas ourselves and by having a repertoire of thinking strategies at our fingertips.

Module 59

Classroom tips

So at this basic level of encouragement:

▶ Cultivate the attitude of enquiry. Never be afraid to say to a pupil 'I don't know the answer. But how might we find out?'

▶ Develop the habit of checking language against its possible meaning. Do this by asking a pupil what is going on in her head as she reads/listens to pieces of language. For insights on how to do this refer to the notion of **metacognition** (in **Having ideas (Module 55)**) and **Visualizations (Module 20)**.

▶ Be nosy about what the pupils write. Seek to know more. Ask questions with your 'thinking agenda' in mind. Saying to a pupil 'That's a really interesting description. How did you think of it?' encourages reflection. Questions like 'But how could that character possibly get up on the roof?' prompt a pupil to analyse the logical structure of the narrative.

▶ Always be supportive. It has been said that a piece of writing is someone's heart in someone else's hands, and even the most (apparently) confident pupils can be bruised.

A few tips

Writing adventure

During our adventure some of the writing you do will be at school and some might be at home. Wherever you write, your teacher and I want you to enjoy making up stories. We think that when you enjoy it you will naturally do your best. I had a friend who was a writer (sadly he has died now), but he always said that getting up to do a day's writing felt like the first morning of a holiday. Imagine that! Well, maybe you won't feel quite so excited – although perhaps you will. But what's important is that you gain pleasure from the writing you do.

Useful writing tips

▶ If you expect to enjoy it you probably will.

▶ What you write is always more important than how much you write.

▶ If you feel stuck and don't know what to write, take a break. If you have to be sitting quietly in class 'getting on with it', just put your pen or pencil down (or take your fingers off the computer keyboard) and sit back for a minute. Let your mind settle. If you have been frowning in concentration or your eyes are tired, rub your hands together to warm them, then cup them gently over your eyes. That's so relaxing. Try it now.

▶ Never be afraid to ask for help. Sincere questions are never stupid. When you ask you are not showing weakness. Asking good questions is a sign of strength.

Take it further

▶ Now hop back to **Getting started (Module 60)** so that you can make your next decision.

Good writing habits

Writers' habits

Many writers and other creatives deliberately introduce a ritualistic aspect to their work, often before the writing begins. Going through the ritual 'gets them in the mood' for the creative flow to begin. Such a mood (though that's not the best word for it) is as much to do with emotion as it is with an intellectual process. It usually involves a feeling of excitement and anticipation, a sense of 'raring to go', a certain inner knowing that 'yes I can do this'. And when the flow begins it is just that, an effortless streaming of ideas and words that seem just to spill out on the page, frequently to the extent that the writer becomes immersed in his own imagined world, lost in the adventure that is unfolding before him. The ease-of-doing is deceptive. In such a mental state the pupil is not snatching at the first thought that comes along or throwing any old words down on paper. He is more likely to be performing at the current peak of his ability and the writing will probably be among his best work (especially after it has been reviewed and refined – see Review notes at the end of the book).

The deliberate 'priming' of the mind and body to perform so fluently makes use of a technique called anchoring. In this sense an anchor is a link that is made on purpose between a particular behaviour/response and something over which you have conscious control. It is, if you like, a switch that you and/or the pupils can flip when you want the flow of writing to begin.

Apparently Ernest Hemingway sharpened pencils to get him in the mood to write. Marcel Proust kept ripe apples in his desk. The sweet smell of the apples triggered the creative flow. Anchors can be kinaesthetic, olfactory (linked to smell), visual, auditory – or a blend of these. You may find it useful to develop a 'collective anchor' when you want the whole class to write. An appropriate piece of music playing in the background prior to the writing session might be most suitable. Or, one teacher I met used aromatic oil to scent the room when writing time was approaching. She was very particular about the oil she selected and, of course, used the same smell each time.

Anchoring for pupils

The pupils might also benefit by establishing individual anchors, something that each pupil can choose to do as a doorway into the writing mood, and also at those points when the right words won't seem to come. I keep a pebble on my desk and handle this (the pebble, not the desk!) when I need to pause and gather my thoughts (see **In the mood for writing** (**Module 1**)). Another useful anchor is to rub the left thumb and little finger together (if you're right-handed, vice versa if left). Encourage pupils to use their anchors also when they feel their writing is going well and also when you offer praise for their efforts. This enriches the link.

Module 58

Good writing habits

Preparing to write

In my spare time I like to cook stir-fry food. Lots of books that show you how to stir-fry say that success is 90 per cent preparation and 10 per cent good cooking. It's a bit like that with good writing, though perhaps the percentages are different.

Some preparation will help you to produce your best work. By that I mean not just your best finished writing, but also your best ideas, notes and first draft. If you take time to prepare whenever you think about your stories and poems you will soon develop a set of good writing habits, which will make life easier from then on. Here are my suggestions:

Useful tips before you start writing

► Make sure you're comfortable. Get the temperature right. Have you got good light? Is your chair comfortable? Do you need to use the toilet? (Go now if you do!) Keep some drinking water nearby. If there are any distractions, what can you do to get rid of them? (If it's your friend who's distracting you, you can't very well get rid of him or her. But you can ask that person politely to leave you in peace).

► Ask your teacher about *anchoring*. This is something you can do to get your brain ready to have ideas. There are also games you can play to create ideas. I'll show you some of these later.

► Concentrate on what you're doing and don't worry about how much other people have written or how good it might be. When I was at school my friend Anthony Morris would always write much more than me and gloat about it! 'Na-na-nana-nah! I've done three pages and you've done only one!' He was trying to wind me up of course, and if I let him (which I sometimes couldn't help) my work was a disaster. So be cool and just take responsibility for yourself.

► Remember that whatever you write it's all part of your learning. Even mistakes are useful if you use them to discover how to do something better.

Take it further

► Look again at the flowchart and decide where you'd like to go next. If you absolutely must go to the toilet, tell your teacher now

A writer's rights

Principles for developing creative thought

In my book *Jumpstart! Creativity* (see Bibliography) I mention what I think are some of the key guiding principles for developing creative thought. Briefly, these are:

The principle of *valuing*

If we ask pupils to think then it is our duty (and more than a duty) to value the outcomes. The ethos of valuing what pupils think encourages them to tackle the greater demands we place upon their thinking as their learning develops.

The principle of *flexibility within a structure*

Narrative forms are structures which, I feel, we should not impose upon pupils too prescriptively, especially during their earlier and probably more faltering attempts. The structures are there to support a pupil's desire to express herself. They should always serve that creative expression and never dominate it.

The principle of *patience*

Pupils' mastery of the various written forms takes time to achieve and can only be cultivated, not forced. Being patient oneself, and encouraging the pupils to be patient as they learn, will lead to deeper understanding and greater competence ultimately.

The principle of *going beyond the given*

That, by the way, is one of the best-known definitions of creativity. Excitement, exploration and experimentation allow learners to master rules and conventions by moving outside them to see what happens. The Japanese haiku poet Matsuo Basho said 'Learn the rules well and then you can bend them.' I think we can add to that by suggesting that bending the rules in the first place is part of that learning process.

Out of these principles I feel arise a number of writer's basic rights. Feel free to add to the list at any time. Note: Some of them have been adapted from the so-called 'Bill of Assertive Rights' to be found in Manuel J. Smith's book *When I Say No I Feel Guilty* – see Bibliography.

Module
57

A writer's rights

A 'right' in this sense means something that you can fully expect to receive. This might mean being treated in a particular way, or doing something that people should not criticise you for. As someone who is learning to improve their writing (as all writers try to do), there are certain things you can expect from other people.

However, rights form one side of a coin. On the other side there are responsibilities. I have more to say about them at the other end of this book, in **A writer's responsibilities** (**Module 2**). You might want to glance at them now. But whether you do or not, there is one responsibility that you must honour above all others – *The responsibility to respect every other writer's rights, just as they must respect yours*.

Writer's rights

Here are some basic rights that I believe to be most important:

► You have the right to learn in your own way.

► You have the right to say 'I don't understand'.

► You have the right to make mistakes, realising that you can learn from mistakes just as much as from doing things well the first time.

► You have the right to change your mind.

► You have the right to accept advice if it helps you to learn, and to reject advice that isn't useful.

► You have the right to judge your own behaviour when you are willing to take responsibility for the consequences of what you do.

What is a story?

If you want to remember what groceries to buy you make a shopping list rather than write a story that mentions those items. When you send a text message to a friend you use shortened words and the other tricks you've learned to save time. If you wanted to explain to someone how to get from the bus station to the town hall, you'd put the directions in a certain order and make sure they were clear and simple.

Purpose

In other words, the form that your language takes is influenced by the job it has to do – by its purpose.

You might think that idea is obvious – and you're right. But it's one of the most important things to learn when you want to improve your writing. Of course you have to know what the different forms of writing are to be able to choose which one is most suitable.

Writing stories

In this book we are concerned mainly with a basic form of writing called story or narrative prose. When people talk about prose (or prose fiction particularly) they usually mean stories. The word 'prose' comes from Latin and means 'straightforward'. I think the idea is that the language we use in a story is clear, simple and to the point. 'Narrative', again from the Latin, means 'to come to know'. So narrative prose is coming to know something in a straightforward way.

And in case you were wondering – as I hope you were – the word 'story' comes from the Latin too, in this case from *historia*. We get the word 'history' from that also and it means 'picture'. So a story is a kind of sequence of pictures that we place in our readers' minds through the power of the words we use.

These ideas will guide us as we count down to being able to write more effectively. But one final point. Some people think that stories and fiction amount to the same thing. In other words, that fiction cannot be fact. Well I don't want to get into a debate about this (mainly because I'm not sitting there with you!). Perhaps it's something you could discuss with your teacher. But I would like to mention that because stories are a great way of sharing experiences and learning about other people, very often they will *tell you something true*.

Take it further

► OK, ready to have some good ideas? Sail over to **Having ideas** (**Module 55**).

Module 55

Having ideas

Teacher's notes

Pupils often say they get stuck trying to have ideas for stories, or else they rely very heavily on material they have already seen or read. There are a number of reasons why this can happen:

Lack of reflecting or metacognition

They have not been taught the skill of **metacognition**, which is noticing and then reflecting upon one's own thoughts. Begin by asking pupils to imagine a pleasant place. You can ask individuals what particular details come to mind. Some pupils will notice shapes and colours very vividly, revealing to you that they are more reliant on visual thinking (others will report they can't see colours at all, or are unable to imagine visually). Some pupils may talk more about the sounds they hear in their imagined place. Others will describe textures and physical feelings – the wind is blowing, the dry leaves are crunching under my feet, etc. In many cases a pupil will do visual, auditory and kinaesthetic thinking but with one mode predominating.

Encourage pupils' metacognition by asking them to mentally see, hear and feel. Find out if pupils are noticing small details within their mental scenario and/or just have a broad overview. Is a particular pupil experiencing the imagined place 'through his own eyes' or looking at himself from a detached viewpoint?

All of these details are important in developing the class's ability to generate ideas. If pupils have difficulty carrying out these mental tasks, practise the skills by using black and white pictures. When the pupils notice small and subtle details, then 'turn up the colours', 'turn up the sounds', 'jump into the picture and touch things'. For more information on this technique see for example my *ALPS StoryMaker* book. Also refer to the Creative Thinking section in *Jumpstart! Creativity*.

Time pressure

Other reasons for pupils' apparent inability to have ideas is pressure of time and/or a competitive ethos in the classroom. Emphasise the importance of thinking time, not just in creative writing but in virtually *everything* pupils are asked to do as part of their learning. Encourage pupils to slow down and enjoy the experience of having and developing ideas.

Being competitive

Competitiveness is a useful and healthy component of some areas of learning, but generally speaking, not in developing young writers' creativity and technical skills. When you want pupils to have ideas explain that you are not asking them to have better ideas than their classmates, but ideas that can turn into stories that they will feel pleased with.

Feeling overwhelmed

The problem of overwhelm. Comments in developing thinking skills in English on the Government's Standards Site include the pertinent point that pupils sometimes struggle because they feel they are faced with too many things to do at once. At the stage of coming up with ideas, emphasise that you are not interested in neatness and accuracy in writing. All you want is for each pupil to have one or more 'seed ideas' out of which their story will grow. It's also important to be clear that you are not expecting the pupils to analyse or evaluate their ideas at this stage. Refining basic ideas occurs as pupils move on in their thinking to look at genre, characters, plot and so on.

Module 55

Having ideas

Coin flip game

Here's a quick game to try. Take a large sheet of paper and draw a straight line across it. Pretend this is the line a story can take. The left end is the beginning of the story and the right end is, well, the end. Write the word 'Danger' somewhere along the line. Pretend that danger occurs in that part of the story.

Apart from that you don't know anything else about your story. Not yet. But now take a coin – a penny is ideal. You are about to think of some questions about the danger that can be answered by yes or no. For each question you ask, flip the coin. Heads is yes and tails is no. Either think of the questions as you go along or make a list now. The kinds of questions you might ask are:

Questions

► *Does the danger happen outdoors?*
► *Does it involve more than two people?*
► *Is it physical danger?*
► *Does it involve weapons?*

Activity

As you learn more, make *short* notes above the line. Look at Figure 2 to see how this works.

Now what else is worth putting in a story?

Some drama, a conflict, some action, a little sadness . . . Use the coin flip game to learn more.

Take it further

If you think you'll use some of what you've learned in your story, go to **Ideas for a reason (Module 54)** first.

Activities

If you want more ideas about having ideas, try these:

► If you have a favourite film or book, talk with your friends about them. Mention the bits that you found especially exciting or scary, funny or magical.

Module 55

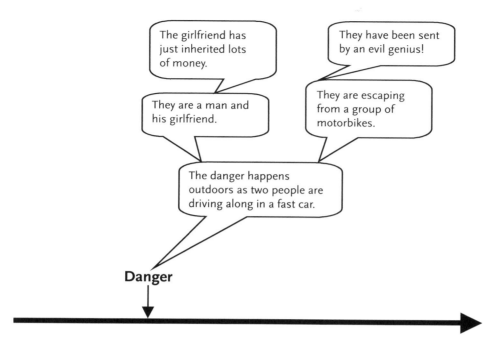

Figure 2 Narrative line and coin flip game

▶ If you think you'll want to write a story based on one that you've read about or seen elsewhere, change it a bit by thinking about the following:

– Introducing a new character of your own. How might that character change the story?

– Think of some 'what if' questions, such as 'What if the hero turned bad halfway through the story?' or 'What if the hero was betrayed by one of his/her friends?' or 'What if the main male characters were female and vice versa?'

Useful writing tip

In other words, play around with the story to see what else you can make of it. The best creative writing happens when you can have your own original ideas, but it's OK to use other people's ideas as you learn.

Take it further

▶ If by now you have a fairly good idea about your story, leap to **Plot, characters and background (Module 52)**.

▶ If you're still stuck for an idea then here are some activities you can try. Go to **Plot bank (Module 53)**.

Module 54

Ideas for a reason

Reflection

Reflection is one of the most important skills a pupil can apply to his writing. Its value is often highlighted by its absence at this early stage of the writing process, where pupils sometimes use the first idea that springs to mind simply because 'it's there'. The problem is compounded by then snatching at other ideas that lead to wildly implausible plots or, just as usually, to pupils painting themselves into a corner plotwise and leaving themselves no way out.

Failure of imagination

This failure of imagination (see Figure 1 on page 5) sometimes occurs in conjunction with pupils using ideas that are very familiar to them, based on a favourite book, film, TV series, etc. The work that arises from this is therefore derivative and unoriginal. I tell pupils that their imagination is like a horse. It's bigger and more powerful than they are, but they are the riders and wouldn't let that horse gallop around wherever it wanted to go. It's fine to run away with your imagination, but you wouldn't want your imagination to run away with you.

The mind naturally produces ideas by making connections. Exploring the connections allows us to decide on the usefulness of an idea or, indeed, whether it works at a basic level.

Testing ideas principle

A simple and effective way of testing ideas is by applying the following principle:

Whatever you choose to use in your work must be there for a good reason that improves the story.

Coin flip game

Insisting on this 'rule of reasonableness' emphasises the notion of authority discussed in the Review. Try out the principle in the coin flip activity explained on page 18. Because potentially the pupils can ask any questions, some will probably ask outrageous or inappropriate questions.

Classroom example

During one workshop session a group was finding out more about the danger at a certain point in the story and had established that it was the hero who was in a dangerous situation set up by the villain. One of the group, John, asked 'Is the hero gay?' I said 'Although we can't control the answer the coin gives us, we are responsible for the questions we ask. Tell me John, if the coin said yes to your question how does the hero being gay improve our story?' John said 'Well the villain can be gay too and decides not to try and kill the hero after all.' I said 'So how will the villain not wanting to kill the hero improve the story?'

The group began to see how the rule of reasonableness worked. Decisions made by the author have consequences that 'ripple out' across the entire story. John realised that his idea was not viable because it weakened the plot rather than strengthened it. *That* was why his question was inappropriate, rather than because it was about the hero's sexual orientation.

This is an important point. Pupils can easily feel criticised or think they look foolish when you ask them to justify the ideas they have. Your intention of course is never to criticise, and the rule of reasonableness never forces you to. Not once do you have to say that an idea is silly or rude (even if you think it is). Simply by asking the pupil to reflect on the idea will lead him to his own conclusions. Giving the pupil responsibility in this way is part of your thinking skills agenda. And of course, if John had been able to make a robust argument for his hero being gay that was congruent with a good plot I would have accepted it and allowed him to use the idea.

Games

Here are two games you can play with the class to encourage them to test out their ideas:

The because game

Explain to the class that 'because' is a *sticky word*. When they use it they have to stick a good reason on to what they say. Begin with a simple situation. Steve was driving very fast along a country lane. Now ask 'Because?' Lots of the pupils will have ideas. Pick one. 'Because he was trying to escape.' Then you say 'And he was trying to escape because?' 'People were chasing him.' 'They were chasing him because?' 'Because he had stolen something valuable from them!' 'And he'd stolen it because . . . ?'

Module 54

And so the game proceeds until you know how the story, or at least that part of it, works. Exploring ideas in this way does not commit the pupils to using them. But it does teach them a method of generating ideas and 'testing' them to see if they build a strong supporting structure for the work.

Note also that this technique also helps pupils to outgrow what I call the 'And then syndrome'. When pupils snatch at first ideas their thinking tends to be a string of and then – and then – and then – and then . . . When you spot this kind of thinking help the pupil to take stock and build reasons into the narrative by saying 'And then – because?'

The if-then game

Asking 'if then' as you explore chains of ideas creates more options and focuses the attention on cause, effect and consequence. Let's have Steve driving fast down that country lane trying to outrun his pursuers. Ask the pupils to suggest something that might happen next. 'He might crash!' Then you say 'If he crashed, then?' A pupil might say 'The people chasing him would catch him.'

At this point you can either say 'And if the people caught him, then?' Or you could go back a couple of steps and say 'Let's suppose Steve didn't crash. What else could have happened?' A pupil might say 'A policeman saw him speeding and set off after him.' Then you say 'And if the police car was after him, then?'

The ideas that you and the pupils come up with can be mapped visually. For each idea think of two possibilities arising from it. More possibilities will make the map unwieldy and very complicated. So each idea grows two if-then branches. This means that very quickly you have drawn a tree-like structure of possible plot lines. Some of them will lead nowhere while others will show potential for further investigation.

Extension

▶ To learn more about this technique see my *Handbook of Creative Learning Activities* – Story Tree.

Ideas for a reason

How can I have an idea?

As you work through the activities in *Countdown to Creative Writing* you'll see that your mind is brilliant at having ideas. In fact, the problem won't be 'How can I have an idea?' but 'Which ideas do I use out of all the ones I've had?'

Games to create ideas

I'm sure you know already that some of the ideas you think of are better than others. By that I mean some grow into stories quite easily while some don't seem to lead anywhere. Your teacher will show you a couple of games that you can play to find out how useful your ideas will be. They are called the *Because Game* and the *If-Then Game*.

Both of these games will help you to understand something that writers feel is very important.

Any idea you decide to use must be there for a good reason that makes the story a better story.

If that doesn't make sense to you yet, don't worry. You'll soon learn how to pick your best ideas out of all the ideas you can have.

Take it further

▶ When you've played one or both of the games I've mentioned, hop back to **Having ideas (Module 55)**.

Module 53

Plot bank

Narrative line

Producing a coherent piece of writing requires pupils to be able to have an overview of the entire story and the capacity to mentally focus on small details. The use of the narrative line (introduced on page 19 and developed in **Narrative lines (Module 38)**) is one way of accommodating both kinds of thinking using a *visual organiser* of information. Major events can be sequenced along the line (using the coin flip technique and/or discussion and decision). These can then be explored in greater detail through, for example, asking small-scale closed questions, perhaps supported by VAK thinking (see **Visualizations (Module 20)**) – What colour are this character's eyes? Imagine this person speaking. What does his/her voice sound like (notice three things, such as speed, volume, tone)? If you had to describe this person to someone, what four details would you choose?

Useful classroom techniques

Prompt pupils to 'focus in' on smaller details by using the visual technique in Figure 3. Take a short section of the narrative line and blow it up to a bigger size. Annotate this line with further small-scale information. Teach pupils the skill of Visualization (see **Visualizations (Module 20)**) which will help them to combine VAK thinking with imagining in greater detail.

Another technique is to show the class a short sequence from a movie and set the DVD to Slow Play/Slow Forward. The action then happens in slow motion, giving the pupils time to notice things in greater detail. A useful workshop is to encourage the pupils to write a detailed description of an event that happens in just a few seconds of 'real time'.

Classroom tip

These techniques can be used with the games explained in the pupil page.

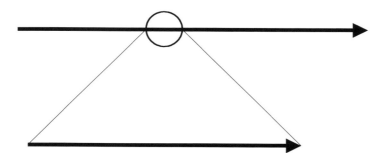

Figure 3 Amplifying the narrative line

Plot bank

Story games

Here are a few games to help you think of ideas for stories.

Have you heard this joke – What do you get if you cross a sheep with a kangaroo? Answer, a woolly jumper. OK, so I didn't laugh much either. But you can use the criss-cross idea to think of stories.

Play criss-cross

▶ Criss-cross two books, or a book and a film. For example, what would you get if you crossed *Charlie and the Chocolate Factory* with *Shrek*? What would you get if you crossed a Star Wars movie with one of Darren Shan's horror stories? What would you get if you crossed a Harry Potter story with a Jacqueline Wilson story?

▶ Make a 'grab bag' of ideas. Ask each person in the class to write down on a piece of paper the name of a character from a story they like. Or an interesting event. Or an object that's important in a story they know. Or a couple of lines of dialogue (speech). Put all the bits of paper in a bag and then draw out four or five and see what you get.

▶ Cut out some pictures from magazines or bits of clip art and stick them on a sheet. Here's one I prepared earlier – Figure 4. Pick two things. If those two things were in your story, what would the story be about? So for example if I picked the mask and the pile of money my story could be about a masked thief who wanted to steal some money. Now pick a third thing (or get a friend to pick it for you). If that were also in your story, what would the story be like now? Keep adding items from the selection until you feel you have a reasonable story worked out.

Take it further

▶ If you want a bit more advice on plotting, disco dance your way to **Plot, characters and background (Module 52)**.

▶ If you're happy with your plot, use your spider-silk to swing to **The structure of a story (Module 47)**.

▶ If you're still looking for inspiration, wiggle your way to **Inspiration (Module 51)**.

Module
53

Figure 4 Grab bag game

Plot, characters and background

Exploring the flowchart

The flowchart explores prose fiction from 'the bottom up', looking at the more basic aspects of story such as narrative elements and genre before investigating the particulars of character and background (settings). This has been done partly for simplicity's sake and to offer young writers a route through the decision-making process of building a story. Some pupils will want to work in this way: out of their big decisions will come ideas for particular storylines, character details and descriptive details of place. Other pupils might have an idea for a specific story in the first instance. A Science Fiction fan for example, being familiar with that genre, may well come up with a number of storylines quickly and easily. When this happens you might direct them to individual modules rather than suggesting they follow the route through the flowchart. Having said that, you might decide that that pupil would benefit from looking at the deeper structure of narrative (elements and sub-elements) to give him deeper insights into his writing.

Using themes

One of the most fundamental aspects of any story are the themes which the narrative explores. These often have their roots in powerful human motivations, feelings and relationships. By themselves they can be rather 'woolly' and abstract – good vs evil, betrayal and loss, altruism, self-sacrifice, the corruptive nature of power, etc. But themes provide the foundation on which a story rests and indeed amount to the *raison d'être* for the story's existence in the first place. The root of the word is the Greek for 'to place' or 'something laid down'. Themes are the basic soil from which all stories grow (see Figure 5).

The notion of themes is only touched upon in the flowchart, in **The structure of a story** (**Module 47**). My intention has been to offer young writers some practical and concrete techniques for getting stuck into a story, rather than to become too involved in abstruse discussion. However, you may wish to spend longer exploring themes with your class (I call them topics when working with younger pupils). Any time spent looking at themes will be beneficial:

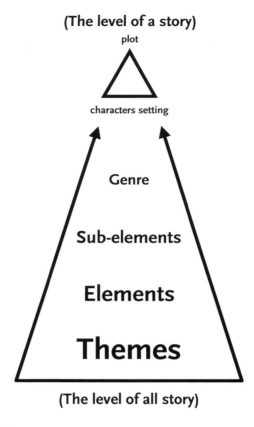

(The level of a story)

plot

characters setting

Genre

Sub-elements

Elements

Themes

(The level of all story)

Figure 5 Levels of a story

▶ An understanding of different themes and how they interact can give rise to endless ideas for stories and poems.

▶ Themes are doorways into the analysis of texts.

▶ Insights at the thematic level help develop pupils' ability to philosophise and thus to link their experience of fictional situations with those that occur in 'real life'. If this idea interests you refer for instance to:

    – *But Why? developing philosophical thinking in the classroom*, Sara Stanley and Steve Bowkett. The pack is a 'starter kit' for establishing a community of philosophical enquiry in your classroom. Intended for KS1 and KS2, the manual comes with four picture books – a dark retelling of *Pinocchio* by Sara and three books by myself – *Philosophy Bear and the Big Sky*, *Dojen the Wanderer* and the poem *If I Were A Spider*.

    – Stephen Law's *The Philosophy Files*. This is a light and humorous but thorough exploration of some basic moral issues such as where do right and wrong come from, should I eat meat, what is real, does God exist and others.

– *The Philosopher at the End of the Universe*, Rowland, M. This is a highly readable exploration of the philosophical issues that crop up in a number of well-known modern Science Fiction films. The book is aimed at adults but will I think offer plenty of talking points you can use with older pupils (and will raise your street cred no end with boys who are into SF).

Module 52

Plot, characters and background

Developing your story

You probably already know that any story includes a plot, characters and background (or setting). I find it useful to think of them in this way:

▶ Plot – what happens and how.

▶ Characters – who makes things happen and why.

▶ Background – where and when things happen.

These are very important words – what, how, who, why, where, when. When you put question marks after these words, they turn into **The six big important questions**. We'll meet them again in **The six big important questions** (**Module 39**) but you can begin using them now.

An example story

For example, let's suppose I was thinking about a story where a masked thief wanted to steal some money (I had this idea in **Plot bank** (**Module 53**)). Asking some of the six big important questions gives me clues about what I still need to find out before I can begin writing my story:

Who is the thief and why does he want to steal money?
Who is he stealing the money from and how will he go about the robbery?
Where is the money kept and how much is there to steal?
How did the present owner come by this money?
Who else might have a claim on the money?
When will the money be stolen?

You see how it works. We also learn from doing this activity that even though you don't have to put all of this information in your story, as an author you need to have thought about it beforehand.

We'll keep coming back to plot, characters and background, but let's move on for now. If you're happy with your plot, hop-skip-jump to **The structure of a story** (**Module 47**). If you're still looking for inspiration, do a silly walk to **Inspiration** (**Module 51**).

Inspiration

Helping pupils be inspired

It is sometimes a great mystery to pupils where authors get their ideas. The question 'What inspires you?' is often asked and provides a good opportunity to look deeper into the matter. The word inspire comes from the Latin 'to breathe upon' and shares its origins with 'spirit'. It is also of course linked with the notion of respiration. I think of inspiration as being the opposite of expiration – of breathing out or breathing one's last as in 'He expired'. Pupils also usually talk about something being 'past its expiry date', which can be apt! More subtly, being inspired is being 'inspirited', being invested with the spirit of a place, a person, an experience. For me inspiration means breathing in the world, feeling alive and motivated to express how I feel, then breathing out that experience as words.

Inspiration is also connected with curiosity and with enthusiasm. These too are fascinating words. Curiosity is inquisitiveness but is linked also with the Latin *cura* meaning 'cure'. That reminds me of a quote by Dorothy Parker 'The cure for boredom is curiosity. There is no cure for curiosity'. The origins of 'enthusiasm' are Greek, from *theos*, which is God; to be infused with the spirit of God. We are back to the idea of 'inspirited'. At its heart, inspiration is a profoundly spiritual experience that amounts to far more than simply having ideas. It is a way of life. My late friend, the writer Douglas Hill, was once asked during an author visit 'Why do you write?' Doug thought about this for a moment and then said to the questioner, 'Son, why do you breathe?'

A triangle of inspiration

In the same way that we can envisage a Triangle of success (**Getting started** (**Module 60**)), so we might imagine a Triangle of inspiration (Figure 6). This becomes a positive feedback loop that is self-reinforcing for the pupils, especially when you create the right emotional climate by showing curiosity and enthusiasm yourself.

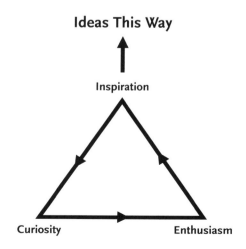

Figure 6 Triangle of inspiration

Module 51

Inspiration

Where do ideas come from?

Do you ever wonder where ideas come from? I think they come from your mind. Experiences go in and ideas come out. Maybe it would be more useful to ask *how* do ideas come from your mind? Really that's what this book is all about. There are lots of ways to have ideas, which are bigger thoughts that you've put together from smaller, simpler thoughts.

But creating ideas is more than just thinking about them. Having ideas is about how you feel as well. When you think of a holiday or your birthday or meeting with your best friends, do you ever feel excited? If you learn some interesting new fact do you ever go 'Wow!'? Have you ever looked at something so beautiful that the sight takes your breath away? That kind of excitement is like the feeling authors get when they are inspired.

Now here's a fascinating thing. You can feel inspired even before an idea pops into your head. It's an excitement and a certainty that you're going to think something great. Then the idea comes along – bang! – and all of a sudden you know what you're going to write about. That same feeling of inspiration can stay with you *as* you write, and what it does is help you to know that the words and sentences are working well, that they're flowing from you as they should.

Getting inspired

So – inspiration is a feeling that helps you to have good ideas and express them well. Inspiration is also something you can do for yourself. Don't just rely on other people to inspire you. Inspire yourself. How do you do that? By being:

Interested
Nosy
Sense of humour (having one!)
Playful
Individual (not just going along with the crowd)
Reflective
Enthusiastic
Determined.

Take it further

Now choose **All of your senses (Module 50)**, **Metaphors (Module 49)** or **'Sounds as it says' (Module 48)** to look at next.

All of your senses

Show don't tell

Advice often given to aspiring writers is 'show don't tell'. For me 'showing' means putting the reader through an experience, and although this exists in the imagination only, because the mind and body are linked, we respond physically and emotionally to the thoughts that authors put into our heads. So, for instance, a funny story works when it makes readers laugh. A scary story succeeds when the reader feels frightened. For a writer to say 'Jeff stood at the top of the steps and felt frightened' is not enough. How do we get the reader's imagination to experience Jeff's fear? (Refer to Figure 7.) Well, the writer can:

▶ Experiment with point-of-view. Imaginatively become the character. Be in his situation. Ask yourself how you would feel to be standing there alone on that dark misty night.

▶ Notice 'internal details' of your physiology as you imagine the situation. A feeling of tension, increased heart rate, faster, shallower breathing, sweating, butterflies in the stomach, a sinking feeling, a chill. Notice external physical details. Eyes wide, fists clenched, shivering with fear and perhaps the cold, mouth partly open, shoulders raised.

▶ Notice multi-sensory details of the environment. Be aware of the particular way the mist is curling and moving. Notice the temperature of the air. What colours can you discern in the dim light of the street lamp? What small sounds just barely break the lonely silence?

Take it further

Note that such 'mix and match thinking' is one version of *synaesthesia*, a cross-referencing of the senses. Learn more by doing an Internet search. Also refer to my *Jumpstart! Creativity* and *100+ Ideas for Teaching Creativity*. Employing synaesthesic techniques is also a useful lead-in to the use of metaphors, as in 'A black ball of fear lay heavily in Jeff's stomach as he stood at the top of the steps.'

My advice is that you work through these ideas with the pupils who choose this module or as a whole-class activity.

Module 50

All of your senses

Let's suppose you were going to write a scene where a character, Jeff, was feeling frightened as he stood at the top of these steps (Figure 7). Your teacher will help you to decide how to write it well.

Figure 7 'Mist and steps' picture (artwork by Stella Hender)

Module
49

Metaphors

Using metaphors

The word metaphor comes from the rich language of Ancient Greece and is made up of *meta*, 'to change and go beyond', and *pherein* 'to bear' or carry. Metaphors have the power to carry us beyond ordinary ways of looking at the world through changing and enhancing the meanings of things. They are sometimes taught simply as one of the common figures of speech; as a comparison along with similes, personification and suchlike. However, the concept of metaphor is fundamental to the powerful use of language.

▶ All language is representational. 'The word is not the thing', but many people react to words *as though they were the things* they spoke of. This is one reason why language is so influential, why the language of persuasion is used extensively in law, politics, advertising, religion and so many other fields of human communication.

▶ Understanding the nature and power of metaphor leads towards deeper insights into symbolic thought itself. Symbolic thought is the (perhaps exclusively human) ability to represent experience mentally and to be able to manipulate those concepts at will. Exploring the value of this capacity goes way beyond the scope of this book, but for instance it allows us to create and benefit from the 'deep meanings' of allegory and myth, to be positively influenced by therapeutic metaphors and so-called 'healing stories'.★

▶ Metaphors can be beautiful and help us to refine our aesthetic sensibilities. They are often created by the unconventional use of language in linking two or more ideas in a way that shocks us out of our routine perceptions. Metaphors thus nourish and strengthen our creative powers, by forging fresh links and generating unusual perspectives.

Take it further

Note that some of the metaphors used in the pupils' section of this module are taken from Dylan Thomas's story *The Followers*.

★ To find out more about this fascinating field see, for instance, *Stories for the Third Ear*, Lee Wallas, *How Stories Heal*, Pat Williams.

Module 49

Metaphors

Using metaphors in your work

Metaphors compare one thing to another. All creative writers use them. They are a method of 'tweaking' our imagination to help us to understand things in different ways. For example in this sentence:

The cold wind howled along the street and bit at my ears.

Can you see what the writer is up to? When you think of something that howls and bites you, what comes to mind? I think of a wolf. The writer (it was me actually) is suggesting that the cold wind is like a wolf. This is not the most original metaphor in the world, but it works quite well because when we make the link between the wind and a wolf, other ideas about wolves pop into our mind and add to the meaning of the sentence.

When I think of wolves I think about hunting, packs, viciousness, beauty, speed, strength . . . So because the wind is like a wolf it is also vicious and fast and strong, and maybe in its own way beautiful as well.

And when I think of hunting I think about cruelty, pain, the laws of nature, predators and prey . . . So the wind is also cruel, painful, predatory but part of the natural world.

So the writer has caused our imagination to do all that work through the use of a simple comparison. That's why metaphors are powerful.

Metaphors are also fun to play with. Take the idea of the wind howling and biting and then change it around in different ways, as shown below.

The wind whispered in my ears and caressed my hair. What does that cause you to think of? What about *The wind skipped and danced and sang around me*? Or *The wind pushed me and punched me and poked at my eyes*?

By changing the metaphor we change the way we think about the wind. We can play the same trick with even fewer words when we talk about the wolfish wind, the kittenish wind or the bullying wind.

Some examples to explore

A poet called Dylan Thomas was brilliant at using metaphors. In one story that he wrote he mentioned *the thistly wind*. How does that kind of wind feel? What about the following?

► Vanilla wind

► Halloween wind

► Penny-whistle wind

► Rugby-scrum wind

► Silken wind.

Another of Dylan Thomas's metaphors is *a pig of a night*. That's quite a common comparison, though when you think about it, it's an unusual idea. What kind of a night is a pig of a night? And why? Pick a few different animals to use instead of 'pig' and ask your friends what they're imagining.

Puddles rainbowed with oil is another Dylan Thomas metaphor. Notice what he did. He took a noun (the name of a thing) – rainbow – and turned it into a verb (an action or 'doing' word) to make his comparison. What is the oil doing in the puddles? It is 'rainbowing'. What pictures come into your mind when you read that? What do you think these noun-into-verb metaphors could mean?

► The children's laughter fireworked across the playground.

► The boys blizzarded into the classroom.

► The party went waterfalling late into the night.

Another Dylan Thomas trick is to invent short descriptive phrases. In his story *The Followers* one of the main characters walks into a pub and sees 'port-and-lemon women' sitting at the bar. What does that phrase do in your imagination? What could it mean? To my mind it means women who are drinking port-and-lemons, but I also think Dylan Thomas is talking about the *kind* of women who sit by themselves drinking port-and-lemons (and if you're wondering what kind of women he might mean, go and ask your teacher about that).

Phrases like these are useful because, again, with a few words they make the reader's imagination do a lot of work. I think it's a technique to use occasionally though and not something to be overdone. Let's try it for ourselves. What are you thinking as you read these?

Module
49

► Pencil-and-glasses schoolkids

► Fags-and-hair roller housewives

► Pinstripe-and-laptop commuters.

What's happening here is that you are being asked to fit an individual (or several of them) into a general type. Such comparisons are often quite humorous – She was all poodles and housecoats / He was all bling and shell suit bottoms / She was all bare midriff and hair extensions. I heard a variation of this idea not long ago when a lady was talking about her partner to a friend and said that he was 'all gong and no dinner'. I'm not quite sure what that means but I think it might be rude.

You'll often find descriptive metaphors that are single words. In his story Dylan Thomas's character meets *an owlish woman*. What do you think she looks like? Notice that the 'ish' ending on the word means 'like' or 'similar to' (an 'ee'-sound ending does the same). What characters spring to mind when you read that one is Rotweillerish while another is kittenish and a third is sparrowy?

We'll come across these little techniques elsewhere in our countdown, but you've probably had enough for now, so jump back to **Having ideas** (**Module 55**) to decide how you'll move on from there.

Module 48

'Sounds as it says'

Creating opportunities for wordplay

As with metaphors, onomatopoeia, assonance and alliteration are often taught as items on the figures of speech checklist. Above and beyond their grammatical qualities these and others offer a wonderful opportunity for wordplay, which I think is an essential aspect of developing pupils' linguistic competence★ and which is congruent with the core aim of this book in helping young writers to be unafraid of ideas.

Drawing meaning from language

Drawing meaning from language is as much an auditory process as it is a visual one. Words are patterns of sound as well as of letters we read. Encouraging pupils to 'roll words around the mouth' helps them to grow more familiar with the language and to own it – language is as much theirs as it is ours or Shakespeare's. Playing with word sounds is but a short step from asking pupils to read their work aloud as part of both the creative phase of writing and during the review. Many writers get the 'feel' that a sentence flows well (or not) by speaking it out: the pattern of the words works partly because the sentence is balanced in the way it sounds.

Perhaps linked to this kind of 'gut feeling' is the process known as pole-bridging, which has been summed up as 'How do I know what I think until I hear what I say?' or 'muttering the understanding'. It is understood by some as being the way the right and left cerebral hemispheres communicate across their linking bridge of nerve fibres, the corpus callosum. During pole-bridging, the subconscious meanings and memories encoded in right-hemisphere neural networks stream across to the left hemisphere where both rational understanding and linguistic processing take place. Here the meanings are articulated and realised by the individual, perhaps for the first time. Muttering the understanding boosts the frequency of 'aha moments' when ideas become conscious.

★ This is what the psychologist Howard Gardner calls *linguistic intelligence*, our innate ability to manipulate information conveyed through written and spoken language. To learn more I recommend Howard Gardner's *Multiple Intelligences in Theory and Practice*. You might also be interested in my thoughts on 'narrative intelligence' in *Success in the Creative Classroom*.

'Sounds as it says'

Exploring sounds

By now you'll realise that I think playing with words is a great way of learning to be a better writer. And of course there are many ways of playing with words – you might already have come across a few of them in your Countdown. Now I'd like us to think about the *sounds* words make when we use them by themselves and in sentences.

Let's look at single words first. Say these words out loud, one by one:

Clank – Buhdoom – Murmuring.

Two of them are probably familiar to you while, quite likely, you haven't seen one of them before. Now think about the following:

► What kind of object might make the first sound (clank)? How did you decide this – in other words, what went on in your head as you thought about the answer? Is *clank* a long sound or a short sound – how do you know? If you wanted to make it into a longer sound how could you change the word? Play about with this idea; you might come up with several answers. If the object you thought about made the sound *clank*, what sound would it make:

1 If it were four times bigger?

2 If it were full of water?

3 If there were ten of them dropped at the same time?

Compare your ideas with those of your friends.

► My brother told me about a place close to where he lives called *Tinkertank Alley*. Why do you think it has that name? If that alley was a place where kids gathered to play marbles instead, what name could we give it then? What if it was a place where mud-pie fights often occurred?

► When you hear the sound *buhdoom* what are you thinking about? If you could measure the 'size' of the sound on a scale of 1–10 (where 1 is a very small sound) where would you put *buhdoom*? Say the word three times slowly out loud. Now say the word *boom* three times slowly out loud. Work with one or more friends to make a list of as many differences between them as you can.

▶ Say the third word, *murmuring*, three times. Notice how you said it. Compare how you said it with how some of your friends said it. What do you notice? If you used the word to describe the wind blowing down the street, what kind of wind do you imagine?

Now don't use the word murmuring at all:

▶ Describe the softest, gentlest wind possible as it blows through your hair.

▶ Describe a huge gusty wind blowing through the trees (do not use *roaring* or *howling*).

▶ Describe a hot dry wind rushing over the desert (imagine countless sand grains stirring and shifting).

▶ Describe a cold gusty wind full of rain as it blows along a deserted street.

Now notice if there are any patterns or similarities in the words you used within any sentence. For instance, my description of the cold rainy wind is:

The wet wind lashed and slapped the leaves, dripped off twigs, washed walls and splashed the pavement slabs.

Now that's not the best description ever, but it's my first attempt. I was able to write it because I imagined myself there on that cold wet street. The things I wrote about are the things I paid attention to in my mind. As I did that, the words kind of suggested themselves. This is what I notice about them:

▶ There are lots of 'w' sounds.

▶ *Lashed, slapped* and *splashed* all have 'l' sounds and short 'a' sounds as in *cat*. The same letters crop up in *walls* and *slabs* – though the 'a' in walls is longer.

▶ *Dripped* and *twigs* have short 'i' sounds as in *kick*.

I think it's better when similar sounds are closer together. By that I mean it helps me as a reader to imagine the scene more vividly. Also by using words that have particular qualities of sound, *we add the dimension of sound of our descriptions*. When I read 'The wet wind lashed and slapped the leaves, dripped off twigs, washed walls and splashed the pavement slabs' I don't just see it in my mind, I can hear it and feel it too.

That's why we learn about alliteration, assonance and onomatopoeia in class. In fact, these are the ideas we're playing with now. If you don't know or have forgotten what those words mean, check with your teacher now.

Module 48

Playing with water

Let's play with water a bit more.

▶ Imagine dropping a small object into three puddles. Here are the three sounds it makes – splish, splash, splosh. How are those three puddles different in your imagination?

▶ Make a list of 'wet' words that contain the letter pattern 'sp'. I think it's very interesting that there are so many!

▶ Imagine a tiny stream high up in the hills. Imagine the water tumbling over the stones. Gradually it becomes a larger river as it flows into the sea. Now imagine again each stage of the water's course to the sea – think about the amount and depth of water, its speed, the way it moves. What words come to mind as you do this?

▶ Say the words *crisp*, *crackle*, *crunch*, slowly three times. Did you move your hands as you said them? How? Why do you think you felt your hands needed to move?

▶ Describe a leather football bouncing down a flight of stone steps.

▶ One of my very favourite poets, Gerard Manley Hopkins, described a blacksmith as he forged 'for the great grey drayhorse his bright and battering sandal'. What do you notice about the words that Hopkins used? Why do you think he put them together in that pattern? (Remember to notice what you imagine as you read the words. That will give you ideas to answer the question.)

OK, we've had a good play with some words. Let's look at how stories are actually built. Splash your way to **The structure of a story** (**Module 47**).

The structure of a story

Pupils' narrative intelligence

In my opinion the best way for pupils to learn about the structure of stories is for them to be exposed to stories of all kinds – not necessarily to be questioned about or asked to analyse or otherwise 'deconstruct' stories constantly, but simply for them to listen, absorb and enjoy. Such learning is called 'osmotic', a soaking-up of insights and implicit (and of course often explicit) understanding of how stories work. Pupils' narrative intelligence (see page 39) will aid greatly in this, though their natural potential for understanding needs to be enriched through varied experience.

It's also useful to note here that increased understanding takes pupils beyond the simple comprehension of stories. In the 1950s, the educationalist Benjamin Bloom devised a way of 'thinking about thinking', a meta-model for classifying thinking tasks and skills along a continuum of understanding. Bloom proposed that retention of knowledge and basic comprehension of ideas (characterised for instance by the ability to restate an idea in different words) are relatively simple ways of thinking, showing little understanding in its deeper sense. Being able to synthesise knowledge – to draw ideas together into a new and complex whole – and to evaluate ideas through experienced judgement that rests on robust criteria of quality, represent advanced thinking reflecting deeper understanding.

When a pupil makes a story (of his own rather than merely retelling) he is in effect demonstrating that 'high order' kind of thinking. Pupils' absorption of hundreds of stories establishes a knowledge base and a platform of experience on which original creation can be based. I also feel that synthesis and analysis are two sides of the same powerful coin. When pupils have practice in making their own stories they become increasingly capable of articulating how stories are put together and how and why they work. This network of skills is *directly transferable* to other areas of the curriculum. So that, for instance, playing with numbers and creating number patterns leads to an increasing ability to analyse mathematical patterns and concepts. Creative writing therefore should never be a token injection of creativity into a literacy programme, but is best thought of as a core activity out of which emerges a wide range of benefits.

Note: For lucid explanations of Bloom's ideas and much other useful information about thinking skills and learning, see *Thinking for Learning* by Mel Rockett and Simon Percival.

Working with different pupils

I think another relevant point to make here is that some pupils can generate an overview more readily than others can. In other words, some pupils have the knack for imagining the Big Picture while other pupils will be better at thinking of small details. The activities in this book can help pupils to take a 'bottom up' approach or a 'top down' approach to story making. That is to say, a pupil with a big vague idea can use that to generate a wealth of smaller-scale information, while someone who has a handful of smaller ideas will learn how to contextualise – to fit them into the broader narrative.

Using the layout of this book

The layout of *Countdown to Creative Writing* mirrors the bottom up approach. If pupils are following the flowchart they are being asked to make big scale decisions earlier on. If 'small chunk thinkers' are having trouble with this then help them to imagine the Big Picture (to have a narrative overview) by:

▶ Summing up stories (in books, films, etc.) in a few words. How in three or four sentences could we describe what *Lord of the Rings* is about? Ask the pupils to tell you about a film that they've watched, summarising the story very briefly.

▶ Linking small imagined details to the greater context. See, for example, the technique of narrative lines in **Narrative lines (Module 38)**.

▶ Play visualization games to enable pupils mentally to 'zoom in' on small details and 'float up' to create an overview. See **Visualizations (Module 20)**.

The structure of a story

Imagining the big picture

Imagine your entire house. Now imagine a room in that house. Now look at the house from the outside and imagine one brick of it. If you can do all of those things, well done because you have the skill of thinking easily about big things and small things. It's a bit like this with a story. When you have an idea for a story do you:

▶ Have a big idea about what the whole story will look like?

▶ Have little 'flashes of ideas' about certain things that will happen in the story, or for example what the colour of a character's hair might be?

▶ Do both of the above?

Being able to do both is useful. But if you tend only to have either big ideas or small ideas, no worries because we'll practise the skill of doing both-big-and-small. Before we go any further though, here are a few guidelines to bear in mind:

▶ If you struggle to have ideas it isn't because you can't have ideas. Our brains are built to have ideas. You just need to learn a few tricks and techniques.

▶ You know that stories have a beginning, a middle and an end. But that's when they're finished. Until then even brilliant and professional authors might not have clear ideas about every part of their story.

▶ Nothing you write is ever wasted. Ideas can be used many times in different ways. Every word you write is helping you to become a better writer if you're prepared to learn from what you do. Doing something 'wrong' is a positive step on the way to getting it right.

Take it further

Now I'll ask you to think about two important aspects of your story – what form it might take and the basic elements it can contain. If your story were a house then the form that it can take might be flat, a bungalow or a mansion. And the elements would be the concrete in the foundations, the metal girders and the load-bearing walls.

If you want to think about the form of your story, somersault over to **Forms (Module 46)**.

If you want to think about the elements of your story, tiptoe across to **Basic narrative elements (Module 42)**.

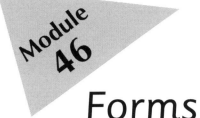

Forms

Form and genre

I want to make a distinction between the form of pupils' writing and the genre within which they can write. By form I mean whether the story will be conventional narrative prose or a series of diary or journal extracts, or letters or text messages or emails, etc. (or even a combination of these). By genre I mean whether a pupil will choose to write a Science Fiction story or a Fantasy story, a Horror, a Romance, a Spy-Thriller and so on. I often come across the use of the word 'genre' to mean genre as I've defined it and 'form', such that someone may speak of the genre of writing diaries or poetry. I think this is unhelpful. The distinction I've made is useful in two ways:

▶ It allows us to separate out the conventions of the form from the conventions of the genre.

▶ It allows us to cross match genre and form as in Figure 8 below.

The conventions of form mean the aspects of the writing that one would conventionally expect to see. So conventionally a formal letter would feature the sender's address at the top right, with the recipient's address below and to the left. The opening greeting, Dear Sir/Madam, etc., would be chosen from a standard selection as would the expected conclusion Yours faithfully/sincerely, etc. That is the form the letter would take.

	Story	Diaries	Play	Emails	Texts	Letters
Science Fiction						
Fantasy						
Horror						
Crime / Thriller						
Romance						
Animal Adventure						

Figure 8 Cross matching genre and form

Module 46

The conventions of genre mean the kinds of characters, settings, situations and other motifs (identifying details) that we would expect to see in, say, an SF story, a Western adventure or a Romance tale. Conventionally one would expect SF stories to feature futuristic technology, time travel, outer space, aliens and suchlike. A Horror story might well include ghosts and haunted houses, vampires and other monsters, etc.

The emphasis here is on what one would usually expect to see. Making a distinction between form and genre allows us to be clearer about the conventions of each. Someone wisely once said 'Learn the rules well and then you can bend them'. So when pupils understand what a Fantasy story conventionally looks like they can begin to play with the rules to create something fresher and more original.

Since you have insight into the pupils you teach, you'll know which young writers need guidance in learning about the conventions of form and genre. You'll also know I'm sure which pupils are experienced and confident enough to cross-match genre and forms and to 'ring the changes' by playing with the motifs of one or more genre.

Cross-matching genre and form might result in a Horror story told through a series of emails, or a murder mystery written as a play, or a Fantasy where text messages have an important function in the plot. More experienced writers might combine two or more forms in the telling of the story. Exploration and experiment of this kind is to be encouraged, but only when you feel it will not lead to confusion.

Module 46

Forms

The shape of your story

Did you know that the word 'form' means *shape*? In this module I'd like you to think about the shape of your story. By that I mean whether the ideas you're thinking about will be written in the way a story usually looks, or whether it will look different somehow.

How could it look different? Well you could choose to write it as a play, or in the form of a diary belonging to one of the characters, or as letters or emails exchanged between different characters.

Take it further

If you're interested in thinking about different forms, you might want to talk with your teacher about it now.

If you're interested in the idea of a 'diary story', flip-flop ahead to **Diary (Module 45)**.

If you'd like to learn about how a play is set out, giant step over to **Play format (Module 44)**.

If you're interested in other forms like emails or texts, etc., zoom to **Letters, texts and other ideas (Module 43)**.

Diary

Keeping a diary

Do you keep a diary? If you do then you'll know that writing in it is like talking to an old friend. If I ever feel angry or upset I write about it in my diary and that helps me to feel better. If something interesting happens to me then recording it means that I remember it more clearly. I think that so many things I see and do and experience would be forgotten and lost if it weren't for my diary.

The word 'diary' comes from the Latin word for *day*, although of course you don't have to write in a diary every day. Think about the kind of writing you would put in a diary. Here's an extract from one of my diary pages.

Wednesday January 16th, 4.50 p.m. (at home).

Today I visited a school in Ipswich to talk about my books, to tell stories and to show the pupils some games to help with their writing. I met loads of friendly people who laughed at most of my jokes. One kid said that he'd already read a couple of my books and liked them. That made me really pleased.

The teachers were very proud of the meals that were served at the school. They were big believers in healthy eating, although there was still chocolate sponge and custard on the menu. I had a big slab of that and could just about eat it all. I dozed on the train on my way home.

Later today I think I'll watch a DVD and make myself a stir-fry for supper (see, I can do healthy eating too!). I'm at home tomorrow and I think I'll spend the day writing.

Notice that the writing is quite informal. That means it's plain, simple and chatty. I don't try to use big words or long complicated sentences. Also because I'm the only one who reads my diary (apart from this extract, which I'm sharing with you) what I say is truthful. And obviously when I write I say 'I' did so-and-so or such-and-such, not 'Steve' or 'he' did so-and-so. This is called writing in the *first person*. Ask your teacher if you're not sure about this idea.

Writing in diary form

If you choose to write your story in the form of a diary, here are the advantages:

▶ You can write informally. In other words your sentences don't have to follow all of the rules of 'proper' grammar. You can shorten words (writing 'I'd' instead of 'I would' for example), but remember that punctuation and spelling are still important – your writing needs to be clear in its meaning because other people will be reading it.

▶ You can get right inside the mind and the feelings of your character (the one who's writing the diary) so that the reader will discover his or her deepest secrets, desires and ambitions. A diary is very intimate in that way.

The main disadvantage of choosing the diary form is that the reader only gets the point-of-view of the character who's written it. I suppose two or more characters in your story could be writing diaries, but that could confuse the reader.

Another option is to write your story in the ordinary way but to include some diary extracts from one or more of the characters. So you could say for example 'It was raining when Steve arrived home. He was tired but pleased with his day. He made a cup of tea then sat in his armchair to write up his diary. This is what it said . . .'

If you decide to structure your story this way you need to know a lot about the different characters whose diaries you feature. You'll learn about characters later anyway, although you might choose to go to **Characters (Module 28)** now. Check with your teacher about this.

If you've made up your mind to write in diary form, hop to **Basic narrative elements (Module 42)** and learn about *story elements*.

If you want to explore other forms you can go to **Play format (Module 44)** to learn about play formats or **Letters, texts and other ideas (Module 43)** to learn about letters, texts and some other ideas.

Play format

Using visual stimuli

The freshness of using a play format instead of narrative prose to write a story can often motivate more reluctant writers and creates opportunities for later performance. The standard play script format springs to mind, but I've found that pupils can also be interested in exploring TV script formats (Figure 9) and radio play formats (Figure 10).

1. **Ext.**   **AT THE RENDEZVOUS POINT.**   **Night.**

> *(Blake stands motionless at the top of the steps, keeping to the shadows. He is obviously nervous. He reaches inside his coat pocket, as though to reassure himself. Suddenly another figure appears...)*

BLAKE: Who are you? Where's Jim?

TULLY (With a throaty voice): Jim has been – ah – detained. You're dealing with me now.

BLAKE: How do I know I can trust you?

TULLY: You don't. Listen, if you don't like it you can walk away now... Or you can ring Davis to check my credentials... Or we can simply do the deal that you arranged. If I mention that I've spoken to Jenna tonight, does that put your mind at ease...?

> *(Blake reaches again into his coat. Tully gasps and turns, as though to run. There is the sound of a single shot being fired).*

2. **Ext.**   **LATER, AT THE WAREHOUSE.**   **Night.**

TULLY: So, Jenna, you thought I wouldn't be coming back...

Figure 9 TV script format

Module 44

(FADE UP EXTERIOR ACOUSTIC: STREET SOUNDS –
PEOPLE WALKING BY, A CAR REVVING AWAY, A
DISTANT POLICE SIREN...)

GIRL: (Sound of her footsteps quickly approaching. She is breathing
               heavily. Sound of her tapping on a window pane). Jonathan...
               Jonathan!

JONATHAN: What? Susan? (Shouts)   I'm on the phone – can't you see that? It's
               important!

SUSAN: So is this. (Sound of her rummaging in her bag)   .

JONATHAN: What's happened? (He gasps)   . What in heaven's name!

SUSAN: I did it for you, Jonathan... Don't you see? If Peter had found out
               about us...

JONATHAN: But a knife – (Shocked and suspicious) What have you done?

SUSAN: Just enough to make us happy, darling.

JONATHAN: No, I won't have this. We were having a good time. But this is
               going too far... No – what are you doing? (Sound of telephone
               handset clattering down). No! NO!

(SOUND OF GLASS BREAKING)

Figure 10 Radio script format

A visual stimulus acts as a good starting point both for developing storylines and
helping pupils to visualize from that point. The coin flip game (see page 18) can be
used to find out more about what might be happening in the picture. And in the
case of the scene depicted in Figure 9, atmosphere and mood are immediately
apparent.

Because TV and radio script formats have a standard layout pupils can quickly become familiar with the conventions of the form. Encourage them to notice and articulate the features of the selected format. Obviously when using the TV script format the writer will need to think visually. Practise this skill with the pupils by visiting **Visualizations** (**Module 20**). The activity called *Filmic Eye* will be especially helpful.

When writing a radio script auditory thinking becomes more important. Emphasise to the pupils that the story must be told entirely through voices and sound effects. With older pupils you might introduce the standard terms for a range of sound effects they might include in their work – see Figure 11.

Take it further

Subsequently recording the radio plays can be great fun, giving the pupils useful experience in controlling the various aspects of the voice – pitch, pace, tone, volume, etc. Sound effects can be improvised (a sheet of thin metal for thunder and so on); alternatively there are thousands out there on the Internet, many of them easily downloadable and copyright free.

> - **Acoustics** – The sound quality of a room or other place. For example 'echoing', 'large open space', etc. You can also say things like 'church acoustic' or 'woodland acoustic'.
> - **Approaching** – The sound is getting closer.
> - **B/G** – Background sounds.
> - **Bring Up/Fade Up** – Increase volume (Similarly 'Bring/Fade Down').
> - **Clean In/Clean Out** – A sudden opening or closing of a scene without fading sounds up or down.
> - **Crossfade** – Blending the sounds of a scene ending with the sounds of the next scene beginning.
> - **Cut To** – Sudden switching of sound to mark a scene change.
> - **Distort** – Instruction that speech is to be distorted somehow, for example over a telephone or loudspeaker.
> - **F/X** – 'Effects', followed by particular sounds needed.
> - **Off (or Away)** – Positioning the speaker away from the microphone.
> - **On (or Close)** – Positioning the speaker close to the microphone.

Figure 11 Radio script terms

Module
44

Play format

Form and format

I'm sure you'll have noticed that the words 'form' and 'format' are similar. 'Format' means 'to form' or to give something a shape. So a play format is the shape or layout your writing takes on the page. There are a few useful play formats you might want to think about.

Standard play format

Usual Format: This is the layout you would use if you intended your play to be acted out on stage. Here's the layout:

▶ Put each character's name in capitals.

▶ If you mention how a character should speak (loudly, shyly, etc.) put a *very brief* direction after that character's name, in brackets and in italics.

▶ Put any stage directions in square brackets and in italics. Keep these directions short, make them clear and simple and separate them out from the words spoken by the characters. Centre them on the page.

For example:

[It is a dark and misty night. Blake is standing motionless at the top of a long flight of steps. He is alone, but shuffles nervously as though expecting someone. Soon afterwards, a shadowy figure appears out of the fog.]

BLAKE: *(his voice trembling)* Who are you? Where's Jim?

TULLY: My name doesn't matter. Jim's not coming. You're dealing with me now.

BLAKE: How do I know I can trust you?

TULLY: You don't. Listen, if you don't like it you can walk away now . . . Or you can ring Davis to check my credentials . . . Or we can simply do the deal that you arranged. If I mention that I've spoken to Jenna tonight, does that put your mind at ease . . . ?

[Blake reaches again into his coat. Tully gasps and turns, as though to run.

There is the sound of a single shot being fired.]

One good thing about choosing a play format is that it cuts down on the amount of writing you do. Also you don't have to remember to use speech marks (inverted commas) around the words that the characters speak – though of course you must use them if you put dialogue into an ordinary story.

TV script

A TV script format looks a bit different. Ask your teacher to show you an example. Notice that:

▶ Each scene is numbered. Ext means external (outside) shot – indoor or internal shorts are Int.

▶ A very brief note of the location is written in capitals and centred. On the right you put when the scene takes place – night, day, evening, etc. All of this is underlined.

There are one or two other differences between a TV script format and standard play format. Can you spot them?

Radio script

A radio script format is a bit more complicated, but maybe you're up for the challenge. Because you're working entirely with sounds you need to keep that in mind all the time. You also need to give enough guidance so that if you or others ever recorded your story, the actors and sounds effects team would know what to do.

Take it further

If you're interested in the radio script format ask your teacher to show you an example layout. You'll see this story starts with a different picture. If you want to practise with these formats try writing a short TV scene based on the picture of the two people waving, and a radio scene based on the picture of the steps at night.

Or if you want to look at other ideas for the form your story can take, march briskly over to **Letters, texts and other ideas (Module 43)**.

If you've chosen your form, learn about basic story elements at **Basic narrative elements (Module 42)**.

Letters, texts and other ideas

Developing disciplines of writing

An important insight into written communication is that the form must fit the purpose. When pupils learn that, for instance, a poem is a poem and not a story, for reasons that the author has previously considered, then an important breakthrough has been made. The teacher's agenda goes beyond that of course. The purposes we have in mind also include finding ways of motivating some pupils to write. We want pupils to develop the disciplines of writing which are an integral part of the craft – the ability for sustained concentration, the active search for effective words, a willingness to review the work so that refinements can be made. Successful writing is the outcome of a network of integrated skills that only evolve when pupils are prepared to sit down regularly and apply themselves. P.G. Wodehouse once advised that the way to become a good writer was to put your backside down on a seat – *every day*. Regularity of practice driven by interest and challenge is the closest thing to a 'magic formula' that we have.

Extension activities

So for that reason over and above any others I look for variety in the writing tasks I can make available to pupils, including modes that initially we might disapprove of. On that basis some ideas to stimulate pupils to write are:

▶ Stories told as a series of text messages between the characters. A more sophisticated development is to have pupils deliberately exploit the ambiguity that can result from such truncated language and/or to build a plot around the misunderstandings that predictive texting could cause.

▶ There's an opportunity here to link the idea of 'text lingo' with a workshop on abbreviations and acronyms and, further, to show how some acronyms are incorporated into the language as words-in-themselves, such as *laser* (Light Amplification by Stimulated Emission of Radiation), where the word itself is familiar but its origins are largely forgotten. Another link is a workshop exploring jargon, where technical vocabulary forms a descriptive shorthand between the users. A paragraph of jargon can be a highly condensed interplay of meanings, or an example of pretentious posing. Exploring these ideas throws up opportunities for looking at the etymology and appropriate use of words.

Finally, playing with text language opens a portal into the whole world of phonics and how we combine letter sounds to create meaning, iykwim? Anyway nuf Z.

▶ Stories as an interchange of emails between characters. These can feature visual backgrounds, pictures, gif files (little moving shapes) and emoticons. They are used to help convey the emotional content of a message. The earliest emoticons appeared as long ago as the early 1880s and were text based, which is to say they were created directly from the keyboard - :-} (smile), :-(0) (yelling), :-}}} (very happy). These days thousands of animated emoticons are quickly and freely available on the internet. As well as pupils incorporating them into 'email stories' you can use them in these ways:

   – Ask pupils to draw or print out sheets of emoticons, cut them out and paste them on strips of paper. The emoticon strips are swapped and pupils make up stories using the emoticons in the order in which they're presented.

   – Put lots of emoticons into an envelope. Have pupils draw them out one by one and make up storylines as they go.

   – Download animated emoticons (that includes smileys, avatars, winks and meegos – and I too was behind the times not knowing what they were!) and encourage pupils to import them into their stories to add fun and colour to the written text.

▶ Consider more ambitious story making. If pupils are working in Word at the computer, they can build hyperlinks into the text. This will take the reader to other pages where, for instance, the same scene is depicted from another character's point of view, or where there is more background information about the characters. The same hyperlinking technique makes it easier to write choose-your-own-adventure type stories.★ In these whenever the reader comes to a point of decision (s)he can choose between two or three alternative courses of action. These are to be found elsewhere in the 'book'.

▶ More ambitious 'multi media' stories can be created as PowerPoint presentations, or through website-builder programs. Pages are connected by hyperlinks and can feature pictures, audio and video. The opportunities here for developing pupils' ICT and Media literacy skills as well as their creativity and writing are enormous.

★ The choose-your-own-adventure format was popularised in the 1980s in a range of successful 'fighting fantasy' stories written by Steve Jackson and Ian Livingstone. These are now reprinted by Wizard Books (www.iconbooks.co.uk). For further details of setting up this kind of writing in class see my *Jumpstart! Creativity*.

Module 43

Letters, texts and other ideas

Exploring and experimenting

Your teacher can give you ideas about different ways of writing your story. So, for example, you might decide to tell it as an exchange of letters between the characters, or as emails or text messages. Another possibility is to use some or all of these different forms of writing in a story that is otherwise written in the usual way.

You will know that there a many forms of writing. The ones I've mentioned are but a few. The point to remember is that each form is suited to a particular purpose or set of purposes. So if someone asked you for directions to the bus station it's not likely you'd make up a poem to tell them the way (there's nothing stopping you of course, but the person who asked might get fed up waiting!).

One of the things we want you to do in this book is to explore and experiment with language – to play with words so that you learn more about them. If you choose to write your story in one of the ways suggested above, then we think you'll be learning more about that form of language. Also, if you don't write stories much then this may revive your interest.

Anyway, talk with your teacher as I've suggested. Then you might want to shimmy over to **Basic narrative elements (Module 42)** to find out about basic narrative elements.

BCNU.

Module 42

Basic narrative elements

The building blocks of a story

Some important insights about this idea were gained by the work of the folklorist Vladimir Propp whose book *Morphology of the Folktale* explores the fundamental building blocks (and variants) of 'story'. These basic narrative elements are:

► **Hero** – a figure representing human strengths and noble qualities.

► **Villain** – an equal and opposite figure representing the 'shadow' side of a person, the mean qualities, evil and selfishness.

► **Problem** – every story features a central problem which the hero must resolve and around which all the action of the story revolves. Subsidiary problems arise as a consequence of the heroic struggle towards resolution.

► **Journey** – the hero moves from ordinary and familiar circumstances to an unknown and dangerous realm of challenges and tests. The journey is literal, often to exotic lands, but also symbolic as the hero's goodness is tested to the limit.

► **Partner** – the use of a partner for the hero and/or villain introduces dialogue and sub-plotting as natural consequences. A partner can also serve as a 'sounding board' for the principal characters and/or represent a sublimated aspect of their personality.

► **Help** – the element of help can serve to introduce new characters, reveal the flaws of the gods (who have their favourites), highlight the mortality of the principal characters, etc. Scenes of danger, daring and rescue are also highly dramatic and sustain reader interest.

► **Knowledge and power** – in knowledge lies power, when it is wisely applied. This is of itself a powerful theme. In many stories the element means the gaining and losing of the advantage through further knowledge. This keeps the narrative interesting and is a vital component in soap operas – watch a few to check (as if you don't already!).

► **Object** – a powerful/valuable physical object often forms the focus of the villain's motives, the hero's journey and the resolution of the central problem. But always implicit in a good story is the symbolic object of the hero's quest, to defeat the villain, resolve the problem and restore balance and normality.

I tell pupils that the more of these elements they put in a story, the better the story will 'work'. Similarly, if any of these elements are left out, the story will suffer and may not work at all. When pupils know about these basic elements they can plan their stories in greater detail by building on this solid foundation.

Module 42

Incidentally, knowledge of these elements can be used as an analytical tool in the exploration of other texts. For more ideas on this as well as referring to Propp you might be interested in Stuart Voytilla's *Myth and the Movies: discovering the mythic structure of 50 unforgettable films*. A further useful sourcebook is Christopher Booker's *The Seven Basic Plots: why we tell stories* (see Bibliography).

Understanding the basic narrative elements

These offer a wealth of useful insights and ideas applicable across all key stages, though of course you will need to tailor any resultant activities or learning materials to the age of your class. In terms of using the basic narrative elements themselves, simply for the pupils to know about them and to have a few examples in mind will be helpful. In this regard see the template below (Figure 12).

Think of a few favourite stories (books, films, comics, TV) and fill in the boxes.

A few of my favourite stories →			
Hero			
Villain			
Problem			
Partners			
Journey (to?)			
Help (who or what gives it?)			
Knowledge and power (who learns something to give them more power?)			
Important object			

Figure 12 Basic narrative elements

Basic narrative elements

Building your story

By 'elements' I mean big, basic important things that you'll put in your story. Many people have investigated how stories are built and have decided that the best stories usually contain the same basic elements. Here they are:

► A **hero**.

► A **villain**.

► A BIG **problem**.

► A **partner** for the hero and maybe also the villain.

► A **journey**. Usually the hero goes on this quest to solve the problem.

► **Help** that is given to the hero and/or the villain.

► **Knowledge** that gives **power**. This is something a character learns that gives him or her the advantage over other characters.

► An **object**, which may have to be recovered, returned to its rightful owner or place, or maybe destroyed.

Your teacher may want you to think about stories you know that feature most or all of these elements. The point is that the more of these you can build into your story, the 'stronger' your story is likely to be.

Take it further

You'll learn more about these elements as you continue with your countdown. All that really matters now is that you know they exist! However, if you want to find out more about them right now, pretend you're an aeroplane and cruise over to **Sub-elements (Module 41)**. Otherwise, let's think about planning your story at **Tips on planning (Module 40)**.

Module 41

Sub-elements

Variations on basic narratives

Vladimir Propp's work uncovered a great range of variations to the basic narrative elements (a simplified list of some of the more common ones appears in Figure 13). For our purposes they are useful in several ways:

▶ Sub-elements create specific relationships between the basic elements of the story. So for instance if *misfortune or lack* appears this may involve the hero or villain with a partner who may be a source of help. Alternatively, one character's 'lack' can give another character an advantage and so on.

▶ This integrative nature of sub-elements helps both to build a narrative and keep it fresh. Different sub-elements can be tried out in combination. Each combination will suggest a different structure for the story. A pupil can work at the level of sub-elements before more specific planning (of events, character details, settings) takes place. Also if a young writer 'gets stuck' for ideas then playing with sub-elements will often generate workable plotlines.

▶ As with an understanding of the basic elements, knowing something of how sub-elements work gives insight into how stories generally are put together, thus adding another analytical tool to the pupils's mental workbox.

Using the sub-elements grid

There are a few activities you can run with the pupils by using the sub-elements grid:

▶ Once a pupil has told you about one or two of her favourite stories and has picked out some or all of the basic elements, look again to see how many (if any) of the sub-elements crop up.

▶ Ask the pupil how she thinks the story might have turned out if different sub-elements had been used, or if one important sub-element had been replaced by another.

▶ Take a well-known fairy tale (*Cinderella* is a great example) and ask the pupils to refer to the grid and spot how many of the sub-elements appear in that story. Emphasise that fairy tales, myths and legends are so powerful because they are built on the solid foundations of basic narrative elements and their variants.

Moving away from familiar territory.	The villain attempts deceit.	The hero is tested.	The villain escapes.	The hero goes unrecognised.	The hero is recognised.
An instruction is given or implied.	The hero or other is deceived.	A helper appears.	The villain is defeated.	A false hero appears.	The false hero is exposed.
A rule is broken.	The villain causes harm.	The hero acquires power.	The situation is resolved.	The false hero makes deceitful claims.	The hero is given a new appearance.
A 'villain' appears.	Misfortune or lack appears.	The hero goes to a new place / to search / for an object.	The hero returns.	A difficult task is proposed.	The villain escapes.
There are consequences for breaking a rule.	The hero is approached with a request or command.	Hero and villain meet in direct conflict.	The hero is pursued.	The task is undertaken.	The villain is punished.
The villain gains information about the hero or victim.	The hero decides on action.	The hero is 'marked'.	The hero is rescued from pursuit.	The task succeeds / fails.	The hero is rewarded.

Figure 13 Sub-elements

► Encourage pupils to choose two or three sub-elements at random to see what storylines suggest themselves. Use a dice to select boxes from the grid. Roll first to count beneath the bottom row, roll again to count upwards – 'along the corridor and up the stairs'. So 4/3 for instance gives us *The hero returns*, while 2/6 gives us *The villain attempts deceit*. The inclusion of randomness in this way prevents pupils from using routine thinking, i.e. being derivative or limiting the scope of their ideas by being too conventional.

Motifs

You'll notice that even at the level of sub-elements we are working in quite an abstract way. *The villain attempts deceit* for instance says nothing about the nature of the deceit or who is being deceived, or precisely why the villain wants to deceive (other than because (s)he's the villain!). The next step in the 'bottom up' approach to story making is to consider more specific motifs. I think of a motif as a 'design detail' that helps to define and describe the broader context. Motifs are usually specific details which hook the reader into a certain situation. A motif may be a descriptive detail of character or place, a piece of dialogue, a 'style' of writing fitted to a chosen genre, etc. So, for example:

► His hands reached out to hers across the candlelit dinner table, but she drew back and tearfully slipped the diamond engagement ring from her finger. 'You'll never deceive me again, Neville', Joanna sobbed with a note of finality in her voice.

► 'I thought ya was supposed to be the cleverest sheriff this side of Dead Wood Gulch!' Black Jake sneered as he trained both six shooters on the silver star pinned to Connor's shirt. Then the sneer vanished as he heard the click of the deputy's rifle just behind him.

► The alien ships had orbited Earth for a year. There were thousands of them, each one the size of a city. Even in the absence of direct threats the governments of the world had capitulated and gone ahead with the mass destruction of weapons. Now, at dawn on this midsummer day, one of the ships dropped silently through the atmosphere and landed with featherdown lightness at the agreed gathering place in the Arizona desert. Moments later the ship's hatchway opened and the aliens walked out. Around the world humanity gave a collective gasp at the televised pictures of the event. The creatures were remarkably humanlike, all were smiling, and none was above three centimetres in height.

Apart from realising why I'm not (yet) at the top of the bestseller lists you'll note that the use of various motifs immediately creates a familiar context. As readers we recognise at once that the first extract is a Romance, the second a Western and the third an SF tale. The value of motifs is that:

▶ They act like 'story seeds' around which narratives can grow.

▶ They link the broader and more abstract narrative elements and sub-elements to particular situations.

▶ Because most motifs are concrete they aid visualization.

▶ They help pupils to recognise (and subsequently avoid) cliché and stereotyping in stories.

▶ They form a kind of 'narrative shorthand' that cuts down on the amount of writing necessary to establish characters, settings and situations . . . 'Black Jake stepped down from his horse and walked arrogantly towards the swing doors of the saloon' gets the reader to fill in a lot of detail, allowing the author to move the story on.

So in teaching pupils about motifs you can encourage them to notice motifs in films, novels, etc. Link the use of motifs to the study of genre (see **Modules 37–30**). Use motifs in character description. Discuss the use of over-familiar motifs with reference to cliché.

Take it further

Another, simpler, technique is to make a list of words that *suggest* motifs. Cut them out, put them in an envelope and have the pupils draw them out one by one and brainstorm scenes or entire storylines.

The kind of prompts I'm thinking about include – bridge, key, gift, crossroads, beast, shore, blade, theft, disguise, tower, threshold, labyrinth, woods, charm, tree, mark and similar. For more exploration of such motifs see my *StoryMaker Catch Pack: using genre fiction as a resource for accelerated learning*.

Module 41

Sub-elements

Using your imagination

Imagine a jewel like a diamond, a big one. Can you see it in your mind's eye? Can you pretend you are holding it in your hand? Notice all the different facets of the jewel and how they reflect the light. Now if that jewel is one of the basic narrative elements, each facet or face is a sub-element. If this jewel is the Hero in a story, each sub-element reflects a different way of using the idea of 'hero'. So what could happen to a hero in a story (and a hero can be male or female remember)?

▶ He might be tempted by the villain.

▶ He might give up trying to fight, but later gain the courage to carry on battling.

▶ He might turn into the villain.

▶ She might meet someone who can help her.

▶ She might be chased.

▶ She might disguise herself.

Asking the right questions

You can probably think of lots more examples. Each of these ideas is a sub-element; a way of using a basic narrative element. Notice that when we think of a sub-element we are starting to learn more about our story, especially if we ask questions:

▶ How is the hero tempted?

▶ Why does he give up fighting?

▶ What causes him to become the villain?

▶ Who does she meet and how can they help her?

▶ Where and when is she chased?

▶ What disguise does she use?

By asking these questions and making decisions we can add plenty of useful detail to our story. Your teacher can tell you more about sub-elements if you're curious. Now I'd like to show you a couple of cool ways to plan a particular story. Battle your way courageously to **Tips on planning (Module 40)**!

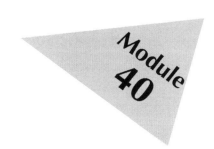

Tips on planning

Planning a story

The degree and nature of planning in pupils' written work has long been a contentious issue. Some authors vehemently advise against planning in favour of just 'going with the flow'. I think this means more than just 'making it up as you go along'. The sustained flow of ideas expressed through writing requires a particular state of mind (see **Good writing habits (Module 58)**) that includes focused attention and sustained concentration. Ideas stream from the creative subconscious and are 'translated' into sentences consciously. The 'processing' of the story (or that scene of it anyway) has been done to a greater or lesser degree 'behind the scenes' and it's now a question of *reaching for the right words* to express whatever is being represented in the conscious imagination.

This way of composing is sometimes called stream of consciousness writing, though as you see I add the proviso that the conscious mind is largely passing on what the subconscious has already thought about. It is one strategy for finding out how a story can develop. What's certainly true is that most writers know more than they realise about the context of the story. The children's author Douglas Hill would notice a scene or character or even a line of text popping into his mind and just start writing whatever came into his thoughts 'to find out more about it'. Years of experience in this way of working often meant that what came out was usually quite polished prose. He told me not long before his death that his latest story had been dictated to him by one of the characters. 'So it's his story not mine,' Doug said, with that wry smile of his that I will always remember.

An important feature of stream of consciousness writing I feel is that to do it well does require long practice. If creative writing is called for under formal (i.e. test) conditions when the pressure is on the ideas might not be 'tight' enough and the story might ramble. So young or inexperienced writers also need clear and effective strategies for planning that allow them to generate and organise their ideas quickly. Such strategies should offer flexibility within a structure. That is, they need to impose method on the task but allow for the pupil to have fresh and creative thoughts. A couple of techniques are explained in **The six big important questions (Module 39)** and **Narrative lines (Module 38)**, and in **Story path (Module 10)**.

Module 40

Further tips on planning

▶ The word 'draft' comes from 'to draw (out)': to draw ideas out of the mind as a rough sketch of some work yet to be refined. Some pupils try and write the story in an elaborated or finished way when they are asked to prepare a draft. This is to be avoided. A draft may be no more than short notes, a mindmap, even a few key words around which further ideas can cluster.

▶ Sometimes reluctant writers can be motivated by the *minimal writing strategy*. Some pupils when they are asked to plan a story just make it up there and then and virtually write out the whole story. In other words they have been trying to compose without much reflection. The minimal writing strategy suggests either that a first draft should evolve out of brief notes (think and make notes before composing) or that the project itself is a short one. Value brevity and choice of words above all else.

▶ Many pupils can suffer from the 'And Then Syndrome' both at the draft stage and in final writing – 'And then . . . and then . . . and then . . . and then . . .' Again this is indicative of 'snatching' at the first idea that comes along. It is routine, linear thinking and the writer probably does not have a clear overview of the whole story and may not have thought about subplots, alternative scenes, endings, etc. A number of the techniques in this book will begin to break that habit. The use of **Connectives (Module 7)**, **Story arcs (Module 11)** and **Flashbacks (Module 12)** show pupils how to refresh and vary their narrative and move it beyond simple and-then linear sequences.

There is a saying in the world of business – 'Plan the work then work the plan'. That's good advice when developing pupils' writing.

Tips on planning

Planning your story

The most important thing to remember is that *the plan is not the story*. The plan is the thinking you do before writing the story down fully. There are really three parts of phases to creating a good story:

1   Thinking time

2   Writing time

3   Looking back time.

This book is mostly about the thinking time, about gathering your ideas before putting the whole story together. It's like going on a holiday. You don't just jump into the car, drive to the end of the street and think 'Now shall I go left or right?' Most sensible holidaymakers pick a destination first and work out their route from a map.

Writing is like that in some ways. If you have a *sense of direction* then at least you have some idea of where you're going. You don't need to know everything about your story before you set out. In fact, being surprised by new ideas while you write is one of the great pleasures of writing. Actually some authors don't want to know how their story ends when they begin writing, because as the story grows they learn new things as they go along, and that leads to the best ending for that tale.

Take it further

If you are writing just for yourself then of course you can take as much time as you like to think before and as you write. But if you are on a time limit then maybe some quick tricks for planning would be most useful.

In that case you might want to look at **The six big important questions (Module 39)**, or drive in top gear to **Narrative lines (Module 38)**.

The six big important questions

Encouraging pupils to ask questions

Encouraging pupils to ask what, where, when, who, why and how familiarises them with an effective strategy for gathering information and exploring alternatives when planning. To launch the technique:

▶ Make a poster featuring a six-pointed star with a question word at each point. Put this in a prominent place in the classroom. Draw pupils' attention to it often (subsequently they will glance at it automatically as a reference). The visual will then easily be remembered when needed.

▶ Use a picture (see Figure 14 as an example) to prompt questioning. Ask the class to think of as many *who* questions as possible, then *what* questions, etc. Build in speculation to explore other possibilities. 'What might that man be doing there?'

   – Maybe he's going to steal the car.

   – Maybe he's waiting to meet someone.

   – Maybe he's an undercover cop. And so on.

▶ Use a picture as a visual analogue for mindmapping – see Figure 15 (colour version available online). Encourage pupils to ask the '6BIQs' and arrange the information accordingly, bearing in mind the four main elements of the technique:

1 Different kinds of information are arranged in different areas of the visual field.

2 The information is colour-coded for easy access.

3 Key words form 'nodes' around which information gathers (the question words themselves are the key words).

4 Encourage links between previously disparate pieces of information.

Figure 14 'Under the bridge' picture

Questions to ask

Emphasis on this final point can generate storylines and scenarios very quickly. Ask questions such as:

▶ What might one link be between the moonlit night and the man on the street?

▶ How can we link the notice pinned to the wall and the man's furtive expression?

▶ How might the tall spire in the background be linked with the strangely swirling clouds around the moon?

▶ What links can we make between the bottle leaning against the barrel and the small bag that the man is clutching?

Module
39

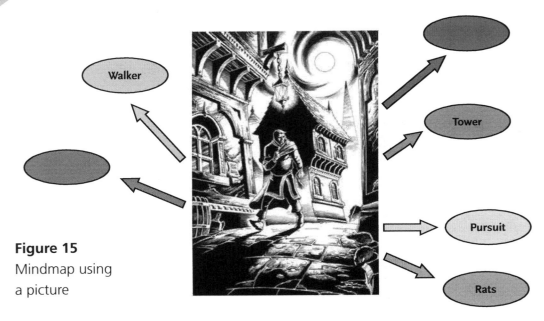

Figure 15
Mindmap using
a picture

Transfer these questioning skills from pictures to text:

> 'Gilly,' said Miss Todd, tilting her head towards the passenger in the back seat, 'I really need to feel that you are making an effort for me.'

Who might these people be? What do you think is their relationship? Why might Gilly be sitting in the back seat? Who else might be there (and why)? These simple techniques build pupils' confidence and logical abilities in the analysis of text; and indeed whenever they engage with information in different subject areas.

▶ Combine questioning with the coin-flip technique. It works well with **Narrative lines** (**Module 38**) also.

▶ Encourage pupils to ask the 6BIQs as part of their thinking time. The questions focus attention, generate information and help to dampen down feelings of panic and that sense of 'I can't think of anything to write!' in tests. So for instance if the task is to write a story based on this title – *The Queue* (maybe accompanied by a picture) – then by asking simply:

   – What might happen next?

   – What could have led up to this point/situation?

   – Where and when is this scene happening? (Also, where and when might this scene take place in my story?)

Pupils gain a sense of control over their thinking while realising that once they've decided on some workable answers they have the 'raw material' for the writing they can then start.

The six big important questions

Asking questions

These are – What, where, when, who, why, how? But I guess you knew that already. Writers tend to be nosy and these questions help you to be nosy in very useful ways. Remember to ask these questions often, even if you're not thinking of a story.

▶ If you see a person on the street you can think to yourself, I wonder what that person is like? Where might (s)he be going? What are his/her family like? And so on.

▶ When you are told facts in other lessons, I'm sure your teacher won't mind if you ask a few searching questions. I was working with one class a while ago and they were doing a topic about France. The class teacher said that Paris was the capital of France. Some of the questions the pupils then asked included:

  – Where is Paris in that country?

  – Is there a reason why people decided once to make Paris the capital?

  – Who decides where a country's capital should be?

  – What does a place need to have for it to be a capital? Does it have to be a city? What is a city?

  – What if (for whatever reason) the French people decided they didn't want Paris as their capital any more? Could they change it?

Neither the teacher nor I knew the answers to some of these questions. But that's what learning is all about!

Reflecting on questions and answers

▶ Reflect on these questions when it comes to the *circumstances* of your writing. I know that probably when you do writing for school you have to do it in the classroom, or maybe you're lucky enough to have a space at home. But even so it's worth asking some of **The six big important questions**. Here are the answers I would give:

Module 39

- Where do I like to write? In the same place each time (in my quiet room at the back of the house).

- When do I like to write? In the morning when I'm fresh.

- Why do I write? Most importantly because I enjoy it. But also because I am sometimes asked to write certain things by different people.

- What do I like to write? Horror and Fantasy stories, poems, and books about thinking and writing like this one!

- Who do I write for? Myself first of all, but then for pupils of all ages and for adults, often teachers with an interest in how the brain works.

- How do I write? I have ideas when I can sit quietly and think. I write these in my notebook. When I have lots of ideas organised clearly in my mind I write my first draft on the computer (neater, and easier to edit!). When I've written the whole thing out I wonder what I can do to make it better. Sometimes kind editors help me to do this.

Take it further

Your teacher can give you more tips about using the 6BIQs, or you might want to kangaroo-hop straight over to **Narrative lines** (**Module 38**). See you there!

Narrative lines

How ideas are generated

Generally speaking ideas are not generated logically and methodically. That kind of thinking is the province of conscious awareness and 'left brain' processing. The right hemisphere of the cerebral cortex assimilates information in a more 'holistic' way. It is the pattern-recognising part of the brain and its work is carried out at a more subconscious level.★ The 'video streaming effect' which is characteristic of the state of creative flow amounts to a positive feedback loop between the left and right cerebral hemispheres across the corpus callosum, the bridge of nerve fibres connecting them. Conscious intention stimulates the release of subconscious material in the form of associations, memories and their attendant feelings. These are then consciously recognised (re-cognised, reflected upon again) and the words chosen to express them.

Linear thinking

One difficulty that writers can face is that while consciously we think in a linear way (the beginning-middle-end structure of narrative reflects this), ideas can 'spray up' from the subconscious in any order. Books on creative thinking sometimes assert that creativity is messy, whereas in fact this is just an effect of the conscious recognition of the work the subconscious has done in thinking about the whole piece of work in an all-at-once-together way.

The *narrative lines* technique helps to accommodate this difference in conscious and subconscious thinking. Have pupils draw a line on a large sheet of paper to represent the linear sequence of ideas that will be the final form of the story. If a pupil has an idea about the end of the story he can make a brief note at the right-hand end of the line. If an insight about the middle of the story pops into mind next, he can annotate the middle of the line, and so on. In short, ideas can be organised in sequence as they appear so that the writer increasingly comes to make logical sense of the sometimes apparently chaotic jumble of thoughts that occurs during creative thinking. Note that this planning technique requires minimal writing and avoids the sometimes messy results of scribbling in notebooks.

★ This is speaking very broadly and simplistically.

Module 38

Developing the technique

Consider developing the technique further in these ways:

▶ Use the coin-flip technique (see page 18) to learn more. Write a word like *crisis* or a phrase like *action scene* somewhere above the line. Encourage the pupils to ask yes-no questions to learn more. When they have this information it can be written up in note form above the line, or as narrative prose elsewhere. If you suggest that the action scene led to the crisis later in the story the pupils can ask **The six big important questions** (**Module 39**) about that, then formulate yes-no questions that the coin flip can answer.

Tip: When pupils have amassed a lot of information this way, allow them to refine it by saying 'Look at what you know. If you want to change anything for a good reason that would improve the story, go ahead and do that now.' Later, discuss their rationales for any changes they make.

▶ Encourage the pupils to draw pictures, use clipart, cut pictures from comics and magazines, etc. to make their narrative lines visually colourful and exciting. Make a narrative line with some pictures sequenced along it and blank boxes in between. Ask pupils to think about the whole story and suggest what words or pictures might fit in the empty boxes.

▶ Narrative lines form an effective visual organiser of information. As such they are a good way of remembering more about stories you've read with the pupils. Make a narrative line from a studied text using key scenes, character names, etc. Use words and pictures to create a colourful visual to post up on the wall.

▶ Combine a narrative line with prediction strips. A prediction strip is a linear sequence of words and pictures with blank spaces at the end and/or in between: pupils work out what would reasonably fit in the gaps. See Figure 16. Note that you can include as little or as much guidance as you like along the line. This allows you to differentiate and scaffold the task without having to spend huge amounts of time preparing completely different sets of materials.

Module 38

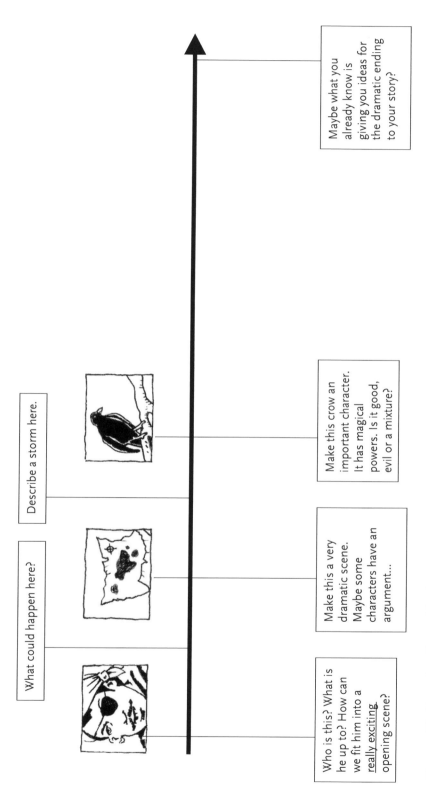

Who is this? What is he up to? How can we fit him into a really exciting opening scene?

What could happen here?

Make this a very dramatic scene. Maybe some characters have an argument...

Describe a storm here.

Make this crow an important character. It has magical powers. Is it good, evil or a mixture?

Maybe what you already know is giving you ideas for the dramatic ending to your story?

Figure 16 Narrative line with pictures

Module 38

Narrative lines

Working out of sequence

A story has a beginning, a middle and an end *when it is finished*. While you are thinking about it ideas might come into your mind any old how. That can be frustrating if you think you've got to work on the start of your story first – but of course you haven't!

It's true that stories need to have a good strong start to get the reader interested. Your teacher will probably have told you that. But sometimes you won't know how to start your story until you've thought about some of the things that might happen later on. Sometimes I'll get an idea for a great ending to my story but don't know yet what happens beforehand. Or maybe a scene will come into my mind and although I know it will go somewhere in the middle of the story I don't know (yet) how that story begins or ends.

It's OK to work like this because that's how the mind often thinks. Your brain is great at having ideas but sometimes they don't seem to appear in the right order. And so a good way of planning a story is to use a narrative line. Look at Figure 17. All the things that will eventually happen in your story can be fitted along the line. But the good thing is that if your first idea is, for example, about the end of the story you can make a note of it at the end of the line. Then as further ideas occur to you, fit them along the line so that you gradually come to know what the whole story will be about.

Remember the six big questions

If you don't have any ideas for a story at all then use **The six big important questions (Module 39)** and either decide on the answers to those or try flipping the coin. Your teacher will explain this if the idea is new to you. Also your teacher can tell you more ways of using the narrative line if you're interested (see Figure 18).

Beginning   Middle   End

Figure 17 Narrative line

Module 38

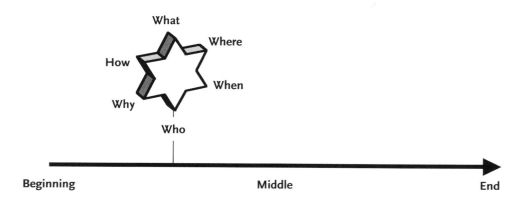

Figure 18 Narrative line and the six big important questions

Well, you've made some very important decisions about your story so far. Now it's time to decide on the genre you want to write in. Put on a very silly hat and get yourself over to **Genre** (**Module 37**).

Genre

Understanding genres

The distinction between genre and form has been made elsewhere (see page 46).
When asking pupils to think about which genre they'd like to write in, the idea of
motifs (page 64) can be useful. A motif is a detail that helps to describe and define
the broader context of the genre. Sometimes pupils – and adults too – become
confused between certain genres. Mixing up Science Fiction and Fantasy is a
common mistake I've met. Helping young writers to be clear about what any genre
might contain is a positive first step in helping them to work at this level.

Another point worth bearing in mind is that genres can be blended to bring
freshness and diversity to stories. So, for example, while Horror and Science Fiction
are distinct genres in themselves, they can be combined to create a horror-story-in-
space. Some 'crossovers' are familiar – Bram Stoker's story of Dracula for example is
a masterful blending of gothic horror and romance. When pupils are familiar with
the basic 'constituents' of the more common genres they can begin to move
towards more unconventional and original ideas.

Useful classroom tips

Some further tips for teaching genre:

▶ Collect generic motifs from books, films, comics and TV (see the notes on
Motifs in **Sub-elements** (**Module 41**)). Create collages of genre-specific
motifs.

▶ Refer to **Ideas for a reason** (**Module 54**). It's easy (and sometimes a sign of
lazy thinking) to drop motifs into a story without reflecting on if or why they
need to be there. For instance, I once read a Fantasy story where a dragon
breathed purple smoke. I assumed I'd find out at some point why the smoke
was purple, but no such explanation was made. I concluded the smoke was
simply a 'special effect' with no purpose beyond an attempt to create an air of
the exotic and the magical. Fair enough as far as it goes, but it was largely a
wasted opportunity. When I used this anecdote with a Y6 class, one pupil said
'It would be better if the dragon breathed different coloured smoke depending
on the mood he was in.' Now that was a *much* better idea.

▶ Remember that genre stories can have depth and power, going beyond mere
entertainment. A great deal of Science Fiction and Fantasy has the quality of
allegory, while Horror is often highly moralistic. Even if you feel that your class

would not be capable of building these deeper layers into their writing, such depths can be explained to them when you look at examples of the genre. So, for instance:

– *The Time Machine* by H.G. Wells is a social commentary on the huge disparity between rich and poor that existed in late Victorian times (what's changed?). Wells used the story to suggest that 'driving poverty underground' would have terrible consequences.

– *The Invisible Man*, again by H.G. Wells, is a parable about the problems that great power can bring. Even though the invisible man in the story could, so you would think, do anything he pleased, his life is one of loneliness and torment.

– *The Monkey's Paw* by W.W. Jacobs illustrates that sinister old proverb 'Be careful what you wish for, just in case it comes true.' Jacobs' prose style looks very dated now, but do improvise the plot as a telling of the story can be very powerful.

– *Frankenstein* by Mary Shelley is another parable of loneliness and the misuse of power. It also raises profound philosophical and moral questions about the nature of life and how far we could justifiably manipulate living material.

There are of course many, many more examples and it's always worth reading genre tales with an eye to the depth and layerdness that some of them will have.

▶ Create narrative line displays (**Narrative lines (Module 38)**) based on well-known examples of genre fiction. Make these as visual as possible so that pupils are exposed to the common motifs of the genres.

▶ Reinforce the basic narrative elements that can form the foundations of a good story in any genre – see **Basic narrative elements (Module 42)**. A hero, villain, problem, journey, etc. can and should crop up in any genre.

▶ Teaching genre creates an opportunity to look at cliché. Many of the motifs in genre tales have now become clichés *because* they are so useful at contextualising a situation very quickly. A useful workshop is to pick out clichés from genre stories and think of more original names/examples/deeper purposes, etc. – see Figure 19.

▶ In Figure 19 the idea of 'cross matching' genres is touched upon. This creative technique can work between and within single genres. Collect motifs from different genres, put them in a box and draw out a couple to cross match. Or use post-its stuck to a board so that pupils can see more possibilities. Play a brainstorming kind of cross matching . . . What do you get if you cross a dragon with a spaceship? Or a wizard with a vampire? Or an android with a Wild West sheriff? Or a romantic dinner between a detective and an arch criminal (the detective doesn't suspect yet!)?

Module 37

Cliché Motif	Genre	More original ideas	6BIQs and Notes
Ray gun / Blaster	SF	• Different coloured 'rays' for different effects. • Sound instead of light – sonic gun. • Hallucination gun that works on the mind. • Think about light in different ways to think of new weapons.	➤ What else could the weapons be called instead of 'blasters'? ➤ Would ray (light) guns work in fog? ➤ Are ray guns the same as lasers? ➤ Would ray gun beams hitting each other cancel out?
Vampires	Horror	• Make vampires good and ordinary people evil. • Make vampires change in different ways depending on the moon's phases. • Put vampires in a wild west story.	➤ Where does the word 'vampire' come from? ➤ What's the difference between 'undead' and 'not living'? ➤ What if you crossed a vampire with another kind of monster? ➤ Can vampires have children?
Observant Detective	Crime / Mystery	• Make the detective a bumbling fool who solves cases anyway. • Cross Crime and Horror – a vampire detective. • Have identical twins as detectives. The fact that people can't tell them apart helps them to catch criminals. • A story where the detective can talk to the animals and they like to help him / her.	➤ Where does the word 'detective' come from and why are they sometimes called 'sleuths'? ➤ Could an intelligent computer be a good detective? ➤ Where did the idea of 'crime' come from? Did the earliest humans have crime? ➤ Will there be new kinds of crime in the future (as cyber-crime didn't exist a few generations ago)?

Figure 19 Using and avoiding clichés

▶ Make up *motif grids* such as the example in Figure 20. Roll dice to choose motifs at random to generate ideas for storylines. Note that grids can also relate to factual topics. In the Ancient Egyptian example below, when the pupils make up stories they will be using and growing more familiar with the vocabulary of the topic you want them to understand. **Tip**: You don't have to fill in all the boxes yourself. Invite pupils to suggest words and pictures to make a whole-class motif grid. For more details of grid work refer to *ALPS StoryMaker* and *StoryMaker Catch Pack* (see Bibliography).

Module 37

Figure 20 Motifs grid (Ancient Egypt)

Genre

What kind of story will you make?

The word genre means 'kind' and is linked with the word 'gender'. When I talk about genre in creative writing I mean the kind of story you want to make. Maybe you like Science Fiction or Fantasy or Horror (these are my favourite genres), or perhaps you're more interested in Crime or Romance or Historically based stories. Some people class Adventure and Comedy as genres, which is fine – but adventure in the form of action and comedy in the form of humour and funny situations can appear in any other genre too. You can have an adventure Fantasy, a comedy Horror, etc.

Most young writers I've met usually have a favourite genre and always try and write that kind of tale. Again, there's nothing wrong with that but part of being a good writer is about flexibility and turning your hand to different sorts of tasks. When I started out as an author I only ever wrote Science Fiction, until somebody suggested that I try other genres too. So I did and it worked. I learned a lot and have had books published in several different genres. So the lesson here is – have fun with the genre(s) you like, but think about trying something new too.

Some helpful tips

Here are a few tips that might help you to explore the idea of genre:

▶ I think that the best stories are written when the author already knows something about the genre. That sounds obvious, but the more you know about what makes a Fantasy story the more ideas you'll probably have for stories of your own.

▶ No matter how much you know about your chosen genre, *keep exploring*. If you like Romance stories keep reading romantic books, watching romantic films, etc. There is always more to learn.

▶ A friend of mine, Pie Corbett, who is a really good poet and writing teacher, uses this helpful formula – *Imitate, Innovate, Invent*.

   – Imitate means to copy the ideas and style of other writers to help you learn. Copying is usually frowned upon, but in this case if you imitate an author

Module 37

you admire you're using that person's work to support what you do. And you will fully expect that by doing this you'll become an independent writer for yourself.

– Innovate means to try new things. You can do that in all kinds of ways. If you have always written Science Fiction stories about battling aliens, have a go at making stories told from the aliens' point of view. If you write Fantasy set in magical realms, try a story where the magic happens in an ordinary town. When you want to innovate, think 'How can I take this plot/these characters in a new direction?'

– Invent means to become more and more original. Inventors already know a lot about the area they're working in, so when they have a new idea it's probably new as far as everyone is concerned (or most people anyway). Inventing new ideas is something you can aspire to and work towards, but your teacher and I will be very pleased if you only imitate and start to innovate. Even the most popular professional writers sometimes never invent a completely new idea!

OK, it's nearly time to look at some genres. I've picked the ones that are the most popular – at least that's what kids in lots of schools have told me. If you know other genres that you would prefer to explore, go and speak with your teacher. Give him/her a bag of sweets and I'm sure you'll get your way.

Before we move on, take a look at Figure 21. It's a brief help sheet that I'd like you to fill in (or at least think about) as you make your next choices.

Take it further

Now use the flowchart to pick a genre. You can look at all of these if you want to, but by the time you reach **Audience and purpose (Module 29)** we hope you'll have definitely decided on one. If none of these suit you (you awkward person!) take a look at **Further ideas for genre (Module 30)**.

Module
37

When you've found a genre that interests you, fill in the parts of this that you can. Fill in any remaining boxes as you continue to develop your story.

My chosen genre is –	It interests me because –
Here are some of the motifs I might use –	
A story in this genre that I like is (book, film, TV) –	
I like this story because –	
Here is at least one way that my story will be different –	
Further ideas and notes . . .	

Figure 21 Genre helpsheet

Module 36

Fantasy

Making the impossible seem possible

Fantasy has been defined as making the impossible seem possible. This is a useful notion because it highlights the importance of believability, not just in Fantasy tales but across the genres. The points made in **Ideas for a reason (Module 54)** can be revisited and emphasised here if a pupil wants to write a Fantasy story. Fantasy enjoys an ongoing popularity in books and films and so it is a rich source of ideas that pupils can build into their own work – see the note on 'imitate, innovate, invent' in the pupils' section on **Genre (Module 37)**. Fantasy also appeals equally it seems to both boys and girls.

Useful classroom tips

To help pupils explore this genre the following points may be useful:

▶ A distinction is often made between High Fantasy and what might be called 'this-world Fantasy'. High Fantasy is the province of exotic realms, wizards, princesses, dragons, the gods, a panoply of outré creatures and beings and spectacular magic. The emphasis is very much on 'the noble quest' and the hero is often a mortal whose courage and daring can startle and sometimes infuriate the gods. The emphasis in High Fantasy can be on romance and/or action and adventure – this is sometimes known as 'sword and sorcery'. Fantasy that takes place in our own everyday world is often more low-key. Out of the commonplace grows the extraordinary. The heroes are usually ordinary children and part of the fascination of the story is about how they deal with the revelation of magic and the new crises and dilemmas that can bring. This-world Fantasy might be an easier option for pupils who are not already familiar with the conventions of High Fantasy (i.e. avid readers of *Lord of the Rings* and (to some extent) the Harry Potter books).

▶ Fantasy in its truest sense is not technological, that being the province of Science Fiction. However, you might find fantastical variations of technology in some stories such as sky-borne galleons kept aloft by hot-hair balloons or pulled along by flocks of albatrosses. Such 'pseudo-technology' can be very exotic and spectacularly beautiful.

Module 36

▶ Fantasy can and often does, however, overlap with the Horror genre insofar as its characters and situations can be 'supernatural'. Is a witch (technically a female wizard) a Fantasy character or a Horror character? The answer is both, depending on how she is used in the tale. Perhaps the use of supernatural beings and situations in Fantasy does not evoke the same controversies that are attached to Horror, where people's sensibilities and religious beliefs might be offended.

▶ A pupil's interest in Fantasy creates an opportunity to introduce or further explore the world of myths, legends and folklore. Here you will find a wealth of plots, characters and settings that can be 'tweaked' to suit a pupil's evolving storylines, or indeed used for straight retellings.

▶ Fantasies can be and often are allegorical, as are many myths and legends. The fantastical happenings in such tales reflect issues, dilemmas, situations and resolutions that are pertinent to our day-to-day life. More sophisticated young writers might grasp the symbolic nature of fantasy motifs. Begin perhaps by looking at familiar tales. *Little Red Riding Hood* is a good example with its moralistic warnings not to wander from 'the straight and narrow path', and where evil appears disguised. Even if pupils don't intend to make their stories into allegories, I think it helps them to realise that genre tales of this kind have depth and relevance in relating to real life in this way.

Note: See Figure 22 Proverbs and fantasy, there are more ideas for using proverbs to develop pupils' creative thinking in *Jumpstart! Creativity*.

Fantasy

Entering a fantasy world

The word 'Fantasy' is related to 'fancy'. Both come from the Greek for 'appearance' and 'imagination'. The idea here is that fantasies are things of the mind, often wild and wonderful in their nature. That gives us a clue about the kinds of things you often find in a Fantasy story – amazing creatures, beings with super powers, incredible lands, wonderful adventures and quests.

There are lots of great Fantasy stories around, both books and films. If you are thinking of writing a Fantasy story but don't know much about the genre, it would be worth asking your classmates what they might recommend you read and watch. Your teacher can give you good advice too.

Some tips to help you

If you know some things about the Fantasy genre and have decided to do a story then here are a few things to bear in mind:

▶ Fantasy stories often take place in magical realms populated by wizards, dragons, evil kings and breathtakingly beautiful princesses. This kind of story is called High Fantasy. But they can equally well be set in ordinary places like your town or city. The children's writer Alan Garner for example has written brilliant Fantasy stories set in Manchester and the nearby Alderley Edge, where he lives. Do an Internet search to find out more about him.

▶ If you intend to write a High Fantasy, where will it take place? What kind of characters will you have in it? Remember what you learned about **Basic narrative elements (Module 42)**. If you haven't visited that module, you might find it helpful to do so now.

▶ Fantasy stories set in our ordinary world can have magic and incredible creatures in them too, of course. Part of the fun of writing such tales is that often the children involved (who are usually important or main characters) have to keep the magical people, creatures or objects hidden from family, friends – and enemies too. If you wanted to write a Fantasy story set in your town, what might it be about?

Module 36

▶ You can get ideas for Fantasy stories (and stories in other genres too in fact) by looking at proverbs. Proverbs are wise sayings or bits of advice – though I find that some are much wiser than others are! Your teacher will help you to find lists of proverbs and explain their meanings. Here are some I like (Figure 22), together with my thoughts about them and how I might turn them into stories.

Tip: You can play the proverb game when thinking of stories in other genres too.

Proverb	What I think it means	Turning it into a story	Other notes and ideas
A bird in the hand is worth two in the bush.	It's better to have something to hand that you can use than more which you can't get hold of.	A dragon chained to a tree is worth two in the sky.	Story about a dragon seller who is asked to find a very special specimen.
A bad husband cannot be a good man.	If you are bad in one part of your life you cannot be good in other parts (but is that true?).	A bad user of magic cannot be a bad wizard.	A wizard uses magic selfishly just once and then has to fight to save his reputation.
A drowning man will clutch at a straw.	Someone who is desperate will take any chance to save himself.	A desperate king will make a deal even with orks.	The king of a land under attack asks help from the nasty Ork Lord.
A rose between two thorns.	Something beautiful and good doesn't change even in the middle of what's ugly and bad.	A white witch between two evil sorceresses.	The two bad witches try to steal the good witch's magic to increase their own power.
Back again, like a bad penny.	Misfortune (in the form of a person or object, etc.) keeps returning.	Back again like a bad wand.	A wizard can't get rid of an evil magic wand that has a mind its own.
Beggars cannot be choosers.	If you are weak and helpless you must take what life throws at you.	Beggars cannot be choosers.	A young elf, abandoned in childhood, joins a tribe of evil trolls to survive.

Figure 22 Proverbs and fantasy

– Finally, if you think you'll use magic in your story don't put it in just because it's easy. Ending a Fantasy story by saying 'The great wizard Zubanallshamalya (or Jeff, if you prefer) swept his wand over the advancing hoard of monstrous orks and they vanished into thin air' is like saying 'They woke up and it had all been a dream.' That's lazy story telling. *If* good magic is going to triumph over bad – and it doesn't have to – at least make the good wizard really fight to win the day. Also, because Fantasy magic is such a powerful force it must be used carefully. Making even small errors with magic can have serious consequences. You have been wand . . . I mean warned.

Take it further

Anyway, jump on board your winged horse and either fly back to **Genre** (**Module 37**) or pick another genre to investigate. May the horse be with you!

Science fiction

Making the possible seem probable

While Fantasy has been called 'making the impossible seem possible', Science Fiction is usefully defined as making the possible seem probable. Most if not all SF (never called 'sci-fi' by aficionados!) explores possible answers to the question *what if*. As such it is essentially speculative, though SF stories range along a continuum of speculation from the wildly unlikely to the almost certainly inevitable.

At the wildly unlikely end are stories that revolve around phenomena and situations which currently seem improbable according to today's scientific knowledge. Thus time travel stories for instance would be placed at that end of the spectrum. On the other hand tales of colonising the Moon and Mars would be classed as 'hard' or 'nuts and bolts' SF and these endeavour to use already existing knowledge and technology as a basis for the narrative.

Pseudo-science motifs

Some motifs that are found in SF serve dramatic purposes above all and, when they are explained persuasively are known as pseudo-science. The famous teleport device in Star Trek (and hundreds of other stories) is simply a convenient way of getting characters quickly from place to place. The same can be said of 'warp drive' that allows faster-than-light travel, although who knows but that one day it just might come to pass.

Science Fiction can also be used effectively in an allegorical way (this point was raised in relation to Fantasy stories in **Fantasy** (**Module 36**)). One of the greats of SF, H.G. Wells, used the conventions of the genre to highlight then-current issues. *The Time Machine*, one of his earliest works, was essentially a nemesis tale where the hedonistic Eloi who lived on the surface of the Earth paid a terrible price at the hands of the underworld Morlocks. These two sub-species of humanity represented the idle rich and the poor labour force, respectively. Wells's book is a beautiful but essentially sinister cautionary tale. So too is his *The War of the Worlds*, which points a warning finger at the complacency of the imperial British exploiting the nations they have conquered.

While most young writers may not be at all interested in using SF as a vehicle in these ways, we as teachers are usefully informed by knowing that the genre has depth and a respectable literary ancestry.

Useful classroom tips

If the pupils are interested only in writing space adventure (also known as space opera) featuring aliens, robots and ray guns then I think that's fine. However, that motivation may draw pupils towards SF-oriented tasks which can develop their thinking skills in various ways.

▶ Play a game of 'what if?' and brainstorm then mindmap ideas. Even an unlikely starting point can lead to rich and scientifically valid discussions. One workshop I always enjoy prompts to pupils to wonder 'what if gravity switched off suddenly and unexpectedly for ten minutes each day?' Simply asking such a question creates an opportunity to talk about gravity, weight, inertia and other scientific concepts in a 'fun' way. If you play this game append these three subsidiary questions:

 – What might the world be like?

 – What problems could we have?

 – How will we solve those problems?

▶ Draw time lines tracing the development of some particular aspect of technology, for instance in communications or transport. Then project that line into the future and encourage the pupils to talk about possible developments. As appropriate, ask them to justify why they think their ideas might come to pass.

▶ Play 'what would the world be like without . . .?'. This highlights the reliance we put on many of the outcomes of scientific and technological progress. What would the world be like without powered flight? Or plastic? Or (heaven forbid!) mobile phones?

▶ One aspect of SF stories is called *the idea as hero*. That is to say, it is the science fictional concept that forms the core of the story while settings and characters can be interchangeable and storylines revolve completely around the one essential concept. The British SF author Bob Shaw once came up with the idea of 'slow glass'. This is glass that, depending upon its thickness, slows the passage of light rays through it to a greater or lesser degree. A 5 mm thickness piece of slow glass, let's say, will release images 'recorded' by the glass a year ago. Once you have found an idea-as-hero in existing SF stories, it's a good challenge to young writers to think of different stories that work around it.

Science fiction

Exploring science fiction

Science Fiction (or SF) as a genre is made up of stories that feature science, scientific ideas and technology in some way or another. Sometimes the science is very 'true to life' and based on what the world will probably be like one day. Other SF stories use ideas that scientists think are less likely. You don't need to know a lot about science to write entertaining SF, but I have found that when I read science books I tend to get ideas for stories as well as learning more about how the world works.

Some tips to help you

A really good way of starting to think about Science Fiction stories is to ask 'what if?' linked to some particular scientific ideas. I'm thinking of things such as:

▶ What if computers could think and actually became cleverer than human beings?

▶ What if you could spend a day in 2108 (or another time of your choice in the future)?

▶ What if scientists contacted intelligent aliens on another planet? What would they talk about? How would the knowledge that life existed elsewhere in the universe affect our lives and beliefs?

▶ What if you invented an anti-gravity machine?

▶ What if you could transfer your personality into an android (a human-like robot) so that you'd never be ill and could exist for hundreds of years?

▶ What if mobile phones were so small they could be implanted inside your head? Just by thinking you could call somebody. And what if the government could listen-in on every conversation that anyone might have?

Another useful way of dreaming up plots for SF stories is to think about the ideas behind SF books and films that you know and change them a bit. In fact, quite a number of modern SF movies have been based on older ideas in this way. Here are a few that I thought of. Note that you might not be old enough yet to watch these movies – I'm only using them as examples.

▶ The Terminator films. Here a soldier from the future is sent back to our time to stop a robot assassin (the Terminator) from killing the mother of a rebel leader who will one day wage a great war against the robots. Change this by making the rebel leader evil and the terminators good. Or maybe the mother lives further back in time, in Victorian Times or Ancient Egypt. Would the Terminator be treated like a god?

▶ *Star Wars*. This is an epic saga about a future space war between the evil forces of the Empire and the freedom-fighting Rebel Alliance. Change this by telling portions of the story from another character's point of view.

▶ *2001: a space odyssey*. This story is about man's discovery of a strange stone-like block on the Moon. It was left there millions of years ago by super-smart aliens. When it was found it sent a signal to the aliens, letting them know that human beings had now reached a certain level of intelligence. Change this by telling what the aliens might do if people deliberately smashed the stone block. Or write the story of man's first encounter with the mysterious alien race.

Finally, I'm sure no one would mind if you used the characters and ideas you already know about from your favourite SF show or film and put them into new stories. Before I ever had my first book published I wrote loads of short stories about Doctor Who and, of course, the Daleks!

Now teleport back to **Genre** (**Module 37**) and, if you haven't decided on your genre yet, from there to one of the other genres.

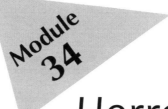

Horror

The different degrees of horror

From years of visiting schools I know that all too often Horror stories can be the bane of an English teacher's life! The dilemma is that Horror might motivate otherwise reluctant writers (usually boys), but the outcomes are often excessively violent, gory and derivative. There is also the issue that revolves around the use of magic and other supernatural motifs. This same problem crops up in Fantasy too, which also makes use of witches, spells and other occult ideas.

Useful classroom tips

It is of course a matter of professional judgement as to whether you ban this kind of material, or use it to exploit the boys' interest as a prompt for them to write. A couple of tricks that I have found to be useful are:

▶ Giving boys who want to write violent stories a few pounds' worth of plastic money. Tell them that they can spend no more than this on violence in their story. Work out what things will cost beforehand. Mention of the word 'guts' might cost 50p. A decapitation will set the writer back £1. Any use of a chainsaw (except perhaps for hedge trimming) will cost £1.50. The point of the technique is to give you control over the pupils' use of violence in their stories and to give them the opportunity to reflect on whether they can achieve the effect of horror without resorting to the crude devices mentioned above.

▶ Find examples in book and film where violent horror is suggested rather than being graphically described. If it's done well the shock effect is actually greater than any explicit depiction of blood and gore. Encourage young Horror writers to emulate these techniques and praise them when they succeed.

Exploring the subtle nuances of horror

In any case the Horror genre is about more than just graphic violence. A glance at any good thesaurus under 'horror' will yield scores of words that suggest the multi-faceted and many-layered nature of both the genre and of human fear. A story whose intention is to evoke apprehension or unease will be very different from the kind of grisly tale touched on above. Exploring the more subtle nuances of horror will serve to refine some pupils' sensibilities and offer them as writers more of a challenge.

I've found that one effective way of working towards finding the words to describe 'gentler' kinds of horror is to use the kind of picture shown in Figure 7 and associated text. Showing not telling is the key. Noticing not just small visual details that evoke mood, but physiological details of the feeling itself gives pupils something definite to write about. When they know what unease (for instance) feels like and how the picture evoked it they will have greater insight as to how to give the reader a similar experience.

Using *artful vagueness*

A handy literary trick in this context is the use of *artful vagueness*. This is where a few descriptive details are used to suggest the object of horror but much is also left to the reader's imagination. Examples of such artfully vague descriptions are:

▶ There could be no doubt that what was moving through the trees was huge.

▶ Stephens watched it loom out of the shadows just for a second, the most frightening face he had ever seen.

▶ She had heard nothing approaching, and even now it made no sound, but she knew it stood right behind her – for its breath on the back of her neck was icy cold.

Also consider the use of comedy when encouraging the pupils to write Horror. Even in 'serious' Horror tales there will be moments of light relief. Our natural reaction after a fright is to laugh (albeit sometimes hysterically), but spoof or comedy Horror is a subgenre in its own right that can sometimes work very well. The style of the comedy can range from outright slapstick to gentle parody. Imagine a lumbering Frankenstein monster landing a job as a supermarket shelf stacker, or a vampire who had read too many health magazines and wanted to turn vegetarian and work on his tan. Or consider the ghost who was desperate to make friends, but couldn't join in with the other kids' games.

Take it further

As with most of the techniques in this book, your own sense of creative playfulness and fun will help the pupils enormously to develop theirs.

Note: If you want some off-the-peg storylines to suggest to the pupils you might look at two books of short stories I've written. *Catch Horror Minitales* (1–85539–174–0) and *Catch SF Minitales* (1–85539–175–9). Both are published by Network Continuum. Each book contains twenty-six short stories with subject matter and language level suitable for upper KS2/Lower KS3.

Horror

Different types of horror

Fear, unease, chill, dread, nervousness, terror . . . All of these might be lumped under 'Horror' and yet each one feels different. It's a bit like talking about the colour red. Take a look around and see how many different shades of red you can find in the next couple of minutes. If you decide to write a Horror story one of the first decisions you must make is what 'shade' of horror to focus on.

Most Horror writers I've met agree that gory violent stories are easy to do. For them the challenge seems to be not simply making the writing more violent but writing about violence in a fresh and original way. Violence for its own sake (in stories or in life) is pretty pointless. If a Horror story is filled with blood and guts it gets very boring very quickly for most readers.

Some tips to help you write horror

I'm talking about this because often learner-writers think that Horror is only about monsters or maniacs jumping out of the shadows and tearing people apart. That's all been done before – done to death you might say. So my recommendation to you is that if you want to have a go at a Horror story and develop your writing abilities explore a different shade of horror. Here are a few ideas:

▶ Can you make your reader feel nervous without mentioning any monsters at all? Can you create a sense of 'chill' just by writing about light and shadows and strange sounds that can't quite be identified?

▶ Can you write a vampire story in such a way that your readers feel sorry for the vampire's predicament? Can you create a believable vampire character who is full of loneliness and sadness because of what he is?

▶ Can you give your readers a shock and a laugh in the same story? In the same scene? In the same sentence? 'Comedy Horror' is very popular in books and films but it takes some skill and imagination to create it. It's great fun though. Can you build up the tension in a scene, deliver a shock, raise a chuckle – then wallop your readers with an even bigger shock? Nothing to stop you having a go.

► Can you invent a new kind of monster that you've never read about or watched in a movie? Or can you take a familiar creature and write about it in a different way so that your story is fresh?

► Can you write a haunted house story with such mood and atmosphere that your readers are filled with tension and *jump* when something suddenly happens? Can your story be so spooky that it will haunt your readers' minds for days to come?

Horror challenges

These are your Horror challenges. If you decide to go for one, then good for you. Talk with your teacher who will show you some techniques for creating mood, atmosphere and tension in your writing. Your thinking about these things will go hand-in-hand with the kind of storyline you select. I've put some plot ideas below. What kind of Horror do you think they suggest?

► A character finds he can begin to read other people's minds. His power develops until what began as a gift becomes a terrible curse.

► A scientist investigates a haunted house and finds to his horror that he has become one of its ghosts.

► The scattered bones of a vampire's skeleton have power over his followers. He commands them to recreate him.

► A guy finds an old bottle on the beach. He opens it and a sinister genie comes out. The genie grants three wishes, but all of them turn out to be nightmarish.

► Some kids explore ancient woodland searching for the legendary Old Man of the Woods. What they find there does not want them to leave . . .

► A girl suspects that the boy she likes is a werewolf. One moonlit night she follows him to the edge of town – where she makes an incredible discovery.

Or maybe you're still deciding about which genre to explore. In which case walk down the long dark hallway and open that creaky old door to **Genre** (**Module 37**). Boo!

Module
33

Crime/thriller

The variety and essence of crime fiction

Crime fiction (adult fiction especially) is an extremely popular genre and, like Horror, has many faces. There is the bleak and brutal criminal underworld kind of story (perhaps not suitable for preteen consumption!) and at the other end of the spectrum the elegant, gently mannered and intricately plotted 'whodunit'. In the same way that some pupils gravitate towards the violent gory end of Horror, so might some young writers think – wrongly – that crime fiction is all about gangsters with machine guns, drugs, bank heists and gung-ho cops who can be as vicious as the bad guys. I think an important part of helping pupils to make decisions about this genre and others is to show them something of its variety and its essence.

Obviously the essence of any crime story is its exploration of criminality. The word derives from the Latin meaning 'fault' and 'accusation'. Crime stories are basically about right and wrong, though these concepts themselves can be slippery depending upon one's beliefs or, indeed, one's particular situation. In what way is it wrong, for instance, for a starving man to steal food from a rich man's table? What if the rich man had gained his wealth by exploiting a downtrodden workforce? What if the thief was stealing food for his starving family? What if the poor man later replaced the stolen food? Would the rich man be right to punish the thief nevertheless?

Discussing morality with pupils

Looking at crime stories creates useful opportunities to discuss the intricacies of morality and where our ideas about good and bad originate. An excellent starter is to be found in Stephen Law's *Philosophy Files*, File 6 Where do right and wrong come from? (see Bibliography).

More immediately perhaps your own thinking about these concepts will throw up ideas for suitable storylines for the pupils to use. Notice how the same question – What if – that proved so useful when looking at SF is again invaluable now.

Motive, opportunity and means

Another 'educational' value of plotting crime stories is that the activity makes pupils think. One central convention of the genre is the use of the MOM device – Motive, Opportunity and Means.

Module
33

▶ **Motive** – Why is the character driven to commit the crime?

▶ **Opportunity** – Where and When can the crime be effectively committed?

▶ **Means** – How can the perpetrator (or 'perp', dude) carry out the crime successfully?

This idea takes us back to **The six big important questions** (**Module 39**). Thinking about MOM can help the barest storyline to develop into something much more interesting. A further refinement is to scatter clues through the narrative so that the reader can try and work out who the culprit(s) might be before they are caught. If they are caught . . .

Useful classroom tips

A quick recipe then for generating a storyline in the genre is to ask the pupils to imagine a crime; a murder, a theft, a betrayal, etc. and to build up the plot details using the MOM device. A story is even more interesting if two or more characters have motive, opportunity and means (a la *Murder on the Orient Express*). And if some clues were to be sprinkled into the plot, what would they be, who would they help to incriminate and where would they best be included? Depending upon the writing experience of the pupils, a couple of red herrings would not go amiss either.

(Incidentally the idea of the red herring, meaning to draw someone along a false trail, apparently derived from the practice of dragging a pungently smoked fish across a fox's path to lead the hounds astray.)

Another way of helping pupils to think of crime stories is to use what I call the CSI Technique (Crime Scene Investigators). There are two versions:

1 Make a list of 'evidence' that suggests a crime and then ask the pupils to fit the evidence to a story. So, for example:

 – A man lies dead in his flat.

 – The windows are all locked. The door is locked from the inside.

 – There are no signs of a forced entry.

 – The open fireplace contains cold ashes.

 – There are wavy marks in the dust on the hearth.

What could have happened? When you have gathered a number of possibilities refine the pupils' ideas with MOM. By the way, the bones of this plot (as it were) come from Sir Arthur Conan Doyle's Sherlock Holmes story *The Speckled Band*.

Module 33

Time permitting, you can make many CSI scenarios based on already existing stories. When pupils tie pieces of evidence together into a coherent storyline they are practising the thinking skill of *hypothesising*. The same skill can be rehearsed in science lessons and other areas of the curriculum.

2   Another variant of the CSI game is to introduce the pupils to a basic crime scenario (perhaps one created by another group) and ask what kinds of clues the criminal might have left. This one is reproduced from my *Jumpstart! Creativity*.

> The cat burglar finished eating his kebab and rode on his motorbike to the other side of town. Parking the bike on a piece of waste ground, he then walked down the street to the big house on the corner. He waited until the rain shower stopped, then climbed over the mossy old stone wall, walked across the flowerbed and hurried over to the window. The window had a wooden frame. He used a tool (decide what) to lever open the window, damaging the frame in the process. Then he crept into the room and walked across the cream-coloured carpet to the cabinet opposite . . .

Once you have settled on a reasonable selection of clues, encourage the pupils to write up the story in more detail (again bearing MOM in mind). The same set of clues can later be presented to another group, who will probably come up with very different plots.

Another convention of crime fiction is the creation and development of a major character (a detective and/or criminal) who appears in a sequence of tales – Sherlock Holmes and Professor Moriarty comprising a classic example. One way of encouraging pupils to think about crime stories is to focus on character creation and then exchange storylines, which can then be adapted to feature a pupil's key character (see **Modules 28–22** on **Characters**). In one school I visited, the pupils ended up writing brief storylines on pieces of card, decorating them and swapping them like trading cards.

Crime/thriller

Right and wrong

Crime stories are about right and wrong. Here is a general recipe for such a story:

► Take a strong need or desire and fold it into a well-described character. This may be the hero, the villain or both.

► Cook over a high heat until the dark side becomes clear.

► Make sure that these characters are more or less equal and opposite. Add twists of personality to taste.

► Sprinkle in a carefully chosen selection of minor characters to give colour and flavour to the dish.

► Splash in a few shocks and at least one generous helping of action.

► Lace with tension, mystery and a little fear. Whisk until these cannot be obviously seen but may take the reader by surprise.

► Pepper the story with clues and other hints. Do not add too many red herrings or you will spoil the taste.

► Simmer with a little passion, envy, hatred, anger or other strong emotion.

► Choose words carefully and keep the suspense on the boil until *well done*.

Some ideas to help you

Your teacher can tell you more about how to think of plots for crime stories, but here are some extra ideas that might be useful:

► Choose a detective that you already know about from books, films or comics and write new stories for that character. Or why not turn, say, a comic book or TV story into a written tale?

► Ask your teacher or a friend to find an interesting-sounding story title that isn't familiar to you. What story could you write that would fit the title? For instance, one of my favourite detectives is Sherlock Holmes. Here are the titles of some Holmes stories. What could you make of them?

  – *The Sign of Four*

  – *The Yellow Face*

- *The Red Circle*
- *The Solitary Cyclist*
- *The Missing Three-Quarter*
- *The Creeping Man*.

▶ Something else you can do is to make up story titles to swap with friends. Personally I like ones that begin 'The Case of . . .'

- The Case of the Broken Coin
- The Case of the Silent Helicopter
- The Case of the Ten Dancing Children
- The Case of the Phantom Cat
- The Case of the Disappearing Classroom
- The Case of the Smiling Supply Teacher.

You get the idea. You'll guess from a couple of these titles that the stories would work well as comedies, or at least be light-hearted rather than serious. Note also that although there may be murders in some crime stories, those tales do not have to be violent. Often the interest for the reader is in the twists and turns of the story and trying to work out who might have done it, rather than relishing grisly details of how the victim died.

▶ Finally, think about telling a crime story within another genre. What if you had a detective who was also a wizard and used magic to solve mysteries? (Hey, that's not a bad idea – I might use that one myself!). Or how about a murder mystery set in the future and/or on a Mars colony? A bit of research to find out what things might be like there will help to make your story more believable. What about a crime-fighting vampire? What about a criminal who is also an alien with some smart technology to help him (or her?).

Maybe you're tempted to have a go at a crime story now. If you think perhaps not, then pucker up and get yourself over to **Romance** (**Module 32**) where you'll learn more about the art of luuurrrvve.

Romance

Exploring feelings and relationships

Because Romance stories tend to be character-led I use this genre with the pupils to explore feelings, relationships and related issues. Although boys tend to be more reluctant to consider writing Romance than girls are they can sometimes be persuaded if the aspects of romantic fiction are embedded in storylines they consider to be less 'slushy'. I point out that in the world of comics, super heroes such as Spiderman, Batman and the Fantastic Four fall in love and, usually, suffer the pain of having to keep their feelings secret or else losing their loved one because of the villain's evil machinations. Most stories in just about every other genre also have their 'romantic interest', while it is the staple diet of TV soaps and other dramas.

Even if you can't tempt the pupils to write Romance it is worth acquainting them with the genre. Writing love stories professionally is a specialist skill and most publishers who work in that field have very prescriptive guidelines about how the narrative must be constructed. The twists and turns of the relationship are carefully plotted and any sexual content and how it is portrayed follows strict editorial rules. In other words standards are high. An author friend has told me that the well-known Romantic publishing company Mills and Boon reject over 99 per cent of the manuscripts submitted to them. The genre remains extremely popular with an intensely loyal readership.

Some helpful introductory texts

For our purposes, stories from series such as *Sweet Valley High* might be introduced to the pupils together with more 'issues based' books by authors like Jacqueline Wilson. Although some of these might not be strictly classed as Romance the genre can be expanded to include them. Any writing the pupils do might be preceded by discussions around the theme of romantic love and the complications that can arise from that – people's jealousy, the notion of rivalry (the classic 'love triangle'), the disapproval of peers, parents, etc. And without stretching the thinking skills agenda too far, exploring the distinctions between true love (whatever that means), selfish love, affection, infatuation and so on will develop pupils' so-called *emotional intelligence*.

Module 32

Useful classroom tips

Here are a few more ideas to try:

▶ **Agony aunt**. Pupils write letters about a range of love-related issues and post them anonymously into a box. Another group/class discusses the issues raised and offers advice. Note: If pupils are embarrassed to have their words read out, even though their identities are secret, 'agony letters' can easily be made up from real examples found in magazines.

▶ **Relationship webs**. These are mind-map-like constructions drawn on large sheets of paper. A number of characters are represented by named dots. Lines are drawn between them and the nature of the relationship is written concisely along the line. So A and B might be joined by a line that is annotated – 'A secretly loves B but feel he is not good enough for her. B thinks A is cute but a bit nerdy. He would be so much cooler if he came out of his shell.'

▶ **Character envelope**. Fill envelopes with miscellaneous small items that indicate the kind of person who owns them. Pupils build a character profile by discussing these. See also the other character creation ideas in **Modules 28–22**.

▶ **Fragments**. Present the pupils with an extract from a Romance story and ask them to speculate about what might have happened beforehand and how the story might develop from here.

▶ **Motives**. Use video clips from TV soaps to discuss the many different reasons (good and bad) why people have relationships. Use romantic scenarios from such dramas as a basis for pupils to write Romance stories of their own.

Romance

A typical romance story

Usually when people think of Romance they have thoughts of luuurrrve. (Pupils always get embarrassed when I say that. I don't know why.) Indeed, Romance stories often are about falling in love and many of them go something like this:

► Boy meets girl

► Boy falls in love with girl

► Girl meets new boy

► Girl dumps old boy

► Old boy feels sad

► New boy dumps girl for new girl

► Old girl and old boy meet again and realise they were meant for each other . . .

Or variations on that theme. But Romance can also involve jealousy, hatred, sadness, self-sacrifice, bravery, petty-mindedness and many other emotions. If we take a broader view of Romance to be about a whole range of different feelings and relationships then that might be much more useful to us – and may make the genre more tempting for you to explore and write.

Think for a moment . . .

Even a few minutes' thought can lead to story ideas, such as:

► An old man near death asks a child whom he trusts to look after his ageing dog after he has gone. Does the child take this on out of affection and loyalty, or is the task a burden and a chore? Does the child come to love the dog as much as the old man did?

► Two children separated by thousands of miles and living very different lives come to know and like each other by being pen pals (or email or text pals).

► A handsome boy at school who wants to get into the school football team dates the daughter of the team coach to help him achieve his ends. A second boy (who really does like this girl) finds out about the scheme. What does he do?

By the way, feel free to change boy to girl and girl to boy in any of these ideas! Romance stories can even fit within SF and Fantasy.

▶ A young sorceress falls in love with a woodsman's son but is forbidden from seeing him because that would weaken her magical powers. These are needed to protect the land against the likely invasion by a truly awful and monstrous enemy (use your imagination). Dare she disobey her parents and mentors?

▶ A scientist falls in love with the image of a woman who lived a hundred years before he was born. He sees her face in a photograph. His longing for her is so strong he invents a transportal to go back through time and meet her and learns to his horror that she was killed on the day the picture was taken. Can he use his time travelling powers to help her? Should he? What would happen if he tried to meddle with fate?

Another source of ideas can be found by watching soaps and dramas on TV. There's nothing wrong with taking a story idea or 'plot thread' and developing it into a story of your own. Something else to bear in mind is that you'll often find so-called 'love interest' in tales from other genres. If Horror or Crime stories appeal to you, could you also weave in some romance to enrich the plot?

Take it further

Your teacher can show you a few more ways for developing Romance stories. Or you might wish to move on to look at Animal Adventures. If so, slink, plod, scurry or gallop over to **Animal adventures (Module 31)** now.

Animal adventures

Personification and animal characters

Broadly speaking animal adventures are stories that either use personified animals as the main characters or feature animals as the central hub of the tale as in the popular *Animal Ark* series of books. Look at suggestions within the other genre modules for developing narratives, bearing in mind that animals will be the focus. Interesting variations on the use of animal characters include:

▶ Using animals as 'archetypes' and have pupils create their own fables about how the fox foxes his enemies or the badger badgers his friends, etc.

▶ Writing new creation tales in the style of Ted Hughes's excellent *How the Whale Became & Other Stories*.

▶ Using character traits attributed to animals as a way of creating human characters. So for instance investigate what it means to be 'catty' about someone. What cat-like characteristics or behaviour gave rise to that metaphor? How could imagining cats quarrelling help us to describe an argument between two people?

▶ Animals-as-people also feature often in stories for young children. Look at storybooks like this with your class. Notice style, language level, conceptual difficulty, etc. and ask your class to write similar tales.

▶ Personified animals are common in Fantasy tales and (though I think to a lesser extent) in SF stories, again sometimes for allegorical purposes. Pierre Boulle's excellent novel *Monkey Planet*, which inspired the *Planet of the Apes* films and TV series, is a fine example. This is an adult read that has the incisive power of George Orwell's *Animal Farm*. More 'child friendly' stories include *Toad of Toad Hall*, Chris d'Lacey's dragon books, *Eragon* by Christopher Paolini, the use of 'daemons' in Phillip Pullman's *Dark Materials* trilogy and many others. In film there is a huge amount of material from the Disney and Pixar studios, the animal/alien characters in Star Wars and so on.

Module 31

Animal adventures

Animals as characters

Animal adventures are adventures with – yes you've guessed it. The adventures might feature animals who are very much like people, or who are still animals but can think and sometimes talk to each other. Sometimes they are ordinary animals but are still important characters

Can you think of some examples that you've read or watched of each kind of animal adventure?

Some useful tips

If you've looked at **Basic narrative elements** (**Module 42**) you'll realise that an animal character can be a – hero, villain, partner, source of help and even important object. Animals can also feature in every other genre, though the genre 'Animal Adventure' usually means that the animal characters are central to the story. Your teacher can tell you more about developing ideas for animal adventure stories, but here are a few to think about right now:

► A development company that wants to buy the land to build a housing estate bullies an animal sanctuary that's struggling to stay open.

► A child is lost and/or gets hurt on a school trip to a forest national park and is helped by the animals living there.

► Pedigree cats (or dogs, etc.) are being kidnapped to be sold on and a group of pupils try to track the criminals down.

► A series of stories about a young detective where animals of various kinds help him/her to solve the cases.

► Consider writing a short story for young children about animals. A few ideas could be The Owl Who Tried to be Wise/Scaredy Cat/The Mouse Thief/The Hamster Family Diaries/The Tale of the One White Crow.

Animal adventures are good fun to write and really stretch your imagination if you want to 'get inside the mind' of a cat or dog or whatever to think about what the world looks like to that creature. I hope you're tempted to explore such tales further. But if you still haven't found a genre that appeals to you then speak to your teacher who can give you a few more ideas.

Module
30

Further ideas for genre

Alternative genres

Less popular genres with pupils (in my experience anyway) include Historical, Westerns, War and Pirates – although fashions can change and as new bestselling books and blockbuster films appear, writing these kinds of tales might catch on a lot more. There is also the option of pupils writing 'mainstream' stories about the lives of ordinary people including themselves and their friends, though remembering to be sensitive to people's feelings, their privacy and the laws of libel!

Inspiring the uninspired

If after sifting through a number of genres some young writers still aren't inspired, then perhaps the following suggestions will appeal:

▶ Write a story using the characters and storylines from a favourite book, TV series or movie. This could be a 'prequel' (what happened before the events of the story you're using), a sequel (how the story you're using might continue), or a parallel tale featuring different characters that are involved in the central plot.

▶ Write a 'What if' story. This can be very down-to-earth (What if no replacement could be found for the lollipop person outside our school?) or fantastical (What if someone invented machines that could respond to your thoughts?).

▶ Photocopy a page or two from an existing novel. Discuss with the pupils what's happening and ask them to think about what could have happened before and what might happen after this point.

▶ Mix and match paragraphs. Take paragraphs randomly from a number of existing stories and ask 'If these were part of one story, what could that story be about?'

▶ Story board. Use a display board in the classroom and invite pupils to bring in pictures, words and small objects to stick on it. If a pupil is struggling for an idea ask him to select a number of interesting items from the board. If these were used in a story what might that story be about?

▶ Comb through newspapers and magazines for items that might spark ideas for stories. TV advertisements can be useful too. Some adverts are mini-stories in their own right that can be developed and written up.

Module
30

▶ Ideas for plots can also evolve out of thinking about characters – see **Modules 28–22**. As a pupil comes to know more about an invented character then asking 'What would (s)he do in such-and-such a situation?' might well give rise to a storyline.

▶ Similarly use story titles to suggest plots. Gather a range of titles (preferably from books the pupils don't know) and brainstorm ideas from there. Try mixing and matching titles too (**Mix and match (Module 15)**) or using a word grid (**Word grid (Module 16)**) to invent some titles that might then act as springboards for developing plots.

Note there are no pupils' pages for **Further ideas for genre (Module 30)**. Once a pupil has chosen a genre direct him/her to **Audience and purpose (Module 29)**.

Audience and purpose

The continuum of literacy

Literacy is commonly defined as the ability to read and write. The educationalist Margaret Meek calls this functional or utilitarian literacy, the basic skills of being able to make sense of the written and spoken word. Literacy ranges along a continuum from, at one end, children (and adults) whose elementary understanding precludes them from appreciating the nuances and subtleties of language – and the tricks that words can play! – to, at the other end, people who can be described as *linguistically intelligent*. The notion of linguistic intelligence derives from the work of Howard Gardner (see Bibliography) who defines intelligence as the potential we have to handle information. This is a powerful idea because 'handle' to me means the willingness and ability to 'get your hands on' ideas, to immerse yourself in the material being studied and used. Handling information in this way allows it to become 'in-formation', that which is being more fully formed into greater meanings and understanding.

Gardner's pioneering work reveals that all of us have the potential to be intelligent in many ways. Our interest lies in linguistic intelligence – the ability to handle information conveyed through language. When pupils are encouraged to play with words, to explore, experiment, test the limits and dare to be bold in an environment where the teacher models that attitude and where ideas and 'thinking outcomes' are valued for their own sake, then opportunities for developing linguistic intelligence are maximised.

This last point is important. The National Curriculum understandably urges the pursuit of high standards of literacy among pupils and various targets and outcomes supposedly reflect their capabilities. If as teachers we agree with Howard Gardner's ideas then our primary goal is to take pupils beyond functional literacy as we help them to appreciate the beauty and power of words and to use language as a life enhancing and life transforming tool.

The literacy framework

The Literacy Framework rightly identifies an awareness of audience and purpose as an important aspect of pupils' understanding of language. Creating stories provides a safe context for the development of abilities that can then be transferred to other and sometimes more demanding fields. If pupils keep in mind who they are writing for and why they are writing as they develop a story, then even that basic awareness will help to form and refine their words.

Audience and purpose

Who are you writing for?

A lot of the writers I've met say that mainly they write stories *for themselves*. 'I write what I like to read' is a common idea. And it's a good one too, because I think that if they tried to write what they wouldn't want to read then the task would be much harder and the outcome less successful.

Your teacher has perhaps mentioned this idea of 'audience and purpose' to you. Your audience is who you are writing for and its purpose is why you are writing it in the first place. If you answer 'to please myself' then you have said something that's both true and wise.

Some useful tips

However, life is a bit more complicated than that – as if you didn't know! If you are writing stories as part of your schoolwork then your thinking about audience and purpose has to take other things into account:

▶ You are writing for your teacher who wants to check that you have learned the lessons he or she has been teaching you about literacy.

▶ You are writing for your parents (or guardians or other 'concerned and caring adults') because I guess they want you to do well and surely you like to feel that they are pleased.

▶ You are writing for your whole school. All of you who work and learn there must feel good when the school is well regarded and has a good reputation.

▶ You are sometimes writing for examiners and school inspectors whose job is to ensure that you meet the standards set out by the government.

▶ You are writing for anyone else who might, by chance or on purpose, choose to read your work.

Now all of this is probably not what your teacher would call 'audience and purpose' as it is explained in the curriculum – I'll come on to that in a minute. But what's important about what I've said is that in most cases when you write you will be making your work public. In fact the words 'public' and 'publish' are linked. When professional authors want to publish their work then they, their editors and other people who are involved work hard to try and ensure that the work is as good as it can be. And your teachers and I are asking you to have the same attitude. When your work is made public it represents you, so we all want it to create the best possible impression.

That attitude is the foundation on which what you actually write is built.

Defining your typical reader

On another level the idea of audience means who your typical reader might be, while your main purpose is to tell an entertaining story. To explore these notions further, read on.

Typical Reader. When I write a story, yes of course, I'm writing it for me, but I also make a picture in my mind of a person who represents my audience. In other words I invent a character who I imagine reading my story when it's finished. To create this character I think about:

▶ Whether this person is male or female. Will you be writing mainly for boys or girls? Or will your story be suitable for either?

▶ How old this person is. This is very important because your decision will affect how complex your sentences are, how complicated the whole story is, and what might be suitable or unsuitable in terms of content.

▶ How much this person knows. By that I mean whether my typical reader might have wide experience of the world and/or of the genre I'm writing in. If I'm writing an SF story for a bright kid who knows a lot about Science Fiction then my story will be different from the same plot written up for an unconfident or inexperienced reader who is only just starting to get into SF books.

You can create this typical reader in your own imagination. If you need help to do it look through the Modules on characters and also the one on **Visualizations** (**Module 20**). Your teacher might also want you to bear in mind other ideas about audience and purpose, but what is really really important is that you *enjoy your writing* and don't worry about all this stuff as the words and ideas pour through your mind.

Now it's time to look at characters. Jump on a trail bike and zoom over to **Characters (Module 28)**.

Module 28

Characters

Creating character modules – general hints and tips

The following modules on creating characters are self-explanatory. General points that may help the pupils are:

► Having said that characters should be consistent, i.e. act 'in character' throughout the story – events also change people. A useful way of developing characters is to ask the pupils how they (the characters) might be different by the end of the story. Combining this with the pie chart technique or the If-Then-Because Game (**A bagful of games (Module 24)**) can help to focus pupils' thinking on this.

► The author Alan Garner says that 'people are like onions – they have layers'. It's important that young writers think about their characters' personalities and backgrounds as well as just their physical appearance. A key character that is simply a name in a story is usually not convincing and fails to create 'hooks' for the reader's imagination to work on. A number of the following activities explore characters in depth.

► It's neither necessary nor even advisable for pupils to put all they learn about their characters into a story. What matters is that pupils are informed about them. When the pupils have created richly woven character profiles encourage them to select the details that will be put into the story.

► It's bad practice to put great slabs of character description into a story. That just holds up the action and readers may well forget a lot of the detail or even skip it entirely. Brief and vivid descriptive details are preferable. Beyond that the characters should be revealed through their (re)actions and through dialogue.

► Character synthesis aids character analysis. When pupils take time to generate and develop characters of their own, they will have greater insight into the motivations of the characters they meet in other stories – in books and films, on TV, etc.

Characters

Three big things

I'm sure you already know that characters are vitally important to the success of your story and form one of the Big Three Things you need to think about, along with plot and settings (or background). Vivid characters help to keep your readers interested and make the whole story more believable and memorable. To prove that, just think of a character from a book, film or TV series that has made an impression on you and who sticks in your mind. If that character had not been so well described or portrayed the whole story might have suffered. Incidentally, while you're remembering this character – why is he or she so clear in your mind? What makes it such a strong character?

Some useful tips

Before we look at how you can make up characters of your own, here are a few basic tips:

▶ Never just have a name for a character and nothing else. If the reader doesn't have at least some idea of what that character looks like then there's nothing for the imagination to work on.

▶ The effort you put into creating characters brings you two benefits. It helps to improve the story you're currently working on *and* you can use those same strong characters again in other stories (though you may have to change the names and a few other details). If you do this you will get to know these characters very well and they will come to seem like old friends – even your villains!

▶ You don't need to put everything you learn about your characters into a story, though the more you know the more believable your characters are likely to be. My advice is to put in only the details that are really necessary for your reader to imagine your characters clearly. Sprinkle these details through the story rather than writing a big block of description.

▶ Pretend to *be* the key characters in your story. I don't mean dress up like them or walk around talking like them (people might think you're odd!). Rather, I mean try and see the world through your characters' eyes. What do they think about? How are their opinions different from yours? What would they think about you?

Module 28

Activities and games for creating characters

In the following modules you'll find lots of ideas for creating characters to put in your stories. I've listed the games below and given each a star rating from 1 to 3. A 1-star game means it's short and simple, while a 3-star game will take you longer, is more complicated and may be more of a challenge for you. Take a look at some of the games to check out what I mean. Also speak with your teacher who will advise you further.

OK, having said all that, let's go and meet some new people . . .

Names (Module 27)★★

SF and fantasy names (Module 26)★★★

Picture a person (Module 25)★★

A bagful of games (Module 24)

▶ Favourite room ★

▶ If-then-because ★★

▶ Matchbox characters ★★★

Character ticklist (Module 23)★★★

Personality profile (Module 22)★★★

Names★ ★

I don't know if you believe that certain names suit certain kinds of people? Choose five first names and ask up to ten people what they think the owner of a chosen name would be like. So for example ask people around school what kind of person Barry would be (although if there is a well-known person called Barry at school this experiment might not work).

Use a dictionary of names

Something else you can do is to look through dictionaries of first names and surnames too if you like. There you will find out the origins of the names, which might help you to suit a name to the personality of your character, or even give you ideas for creating a character in the first place.

Important advice

Below are more tips for naming characters, but first some important advice:

► If you base characters and/or their names on people you know, you must ask their permission first.

► Never write anything nasty about a real person (even if that person actually is not so pleasant!). This big no-no is called libel and leads to all kinds of trouble.

► Don't struggle to think of names. Usually what comes out sounds artificial and forced.

Some useful tips

Instead you might try:

► Looking in telephone directories. Pick a surname (last name) then flip more pages and pick the first first name you see (Does that make sense – the first first name?). TV listings magazines are good for this too. There you'll find hundreds of names of actors and the characters they play. Jot down first names and surnames that interest you and try them in different combinations.

► Go to the library and make two lists, one of authors' first names and one of their surnames. Put the lists side by side and cross-match first names with last names until you come up with some that work well.

Module 27

▶ In real life some surnames originally suggested the owner's job or said something about their character or family. For instance the name Clarke once referred to someone who was a cleric (a clergyman). The surname Martin evolved out of the first name and meant 'of Mars', who was the Roman god of war. Someone with the name Martin might then have been a warrior or had warrior-like qualities. There are hundreds more examples and it can be fun to browse through dictionaries of names.

▶ With the above idea in mind, it's quite easy to invent surnames to fit to certain types of characters. This works particularly well for comedy or Horror characters. For example, I invented an evil surgeon called Doctor Scalpel, a Headmaster with a very loud voice called Mr Boomer, a kid who could run really fast named Jack Sprint, a girl who loved fish called Ann Chovy and a man who hated cigarettes. He was called Nosmo King (think about it).

Tip: You can use the same technique for inventing place names. What do you think Worseborough would be like? Or Maple Street? Or the town of West Foundry? For more ideas see **Settings** (**Module 21**).

▶ Nicknames. The word nickname morphed out of the old term 'ekename', which means an additional name. The 'eke' part means to increase. Nicknames are often affectionate or funny but can sometimes be cruel. I once had a friend who was a really big bulky kid with huge square shoulders. We called him Wall. Another kid had the nickname Limerick because, like a kind of poem called a limerick, he was short and simple. One boy I remember at school was really named Norman, but nobody liked him much and so he was No Man. If he ever asked to hang about with other kids in the playground they would always say 'No, Man'. Get it? Not very nice. Sometimes nicknames are *ironic*, which is to say they really mean the opposite. One skinny kid I came across was known as the Incredible Hulk by his friends. I wonder if the fact he was green and could pick up cars had anything to do with it? Just joking.

SF and fantasy names★★★

Some ideas for creating names

The names of characters in these genres can be weird and wonderful. Here are some ideas for thinking up your own:

▶ Firstly read stories of the kind you want to write to get the 'feel' for the way characters are named.

▶ Sometimes characters in Fantasy stories are named after a physical characteristic – Goldilocks for example. One of my favourite Fantasy stories is Alan Garner's *The Weirdstone of Brisingamen*, where an important character is called Cadellin Silverbrow. Use the trick yourself. How about characters such as Crooknose, Dragfoot, Shinyeye or Fleetglance?

▶ In Fantasy you also find characters and important objects such as weapons named after what they can do. A sword or a person might be called Trollslayer, while a trainer of battle-dragons could be Dragondancer. See how that works? Just push a noun and a verb together. Moongazer, Oakhewer, Gemtaker, Batrustler (OK maybe that's going a bit too far . . .). Just playing this game can give you ideas for stories!

▶ Another version of the above technique combines a verb and an '-ly' adverb. Golightly is a name I've seen before that uses this trick, but how about – Stepsmartly, Sipsoftly, Glancequickly? Try other adverbs and even phrases – Walktall, Jumpsideways, Nagalways (I was thinking of my wife – No not really).

▶ Or keep it simple and think about what you want your character to do. If I create a wizard who makes spells I might call him Spellman. If I create a clever thief I could name him or her Nickit. A cleaner could be Mopnow, a farmer might be Highmeadows and so on.

Playing with words

It's all about playing with words. When you have lots of ideas in this way you're bound to come up with some brilliant ones.

Module 26

► Take an ordinary name and play around with it. Add letters, take letters away, put them in a different order. 'Brian' can become Brin, Bran, Rian, Riana, Arian, Inar, Bron, Obron, Ibor (I've been told that plenty of times!), Borian, Boriana, Nair, Ibran – and on and on.

► Make up futuristic-sounding SF names by spelling an ordinary name slightly differently. So Steve becomes Steev, Anna turns into An-Nah, Paul morphs into Pawl, etc.

► See what happens when you take an ordinary sentence and put the last syllable of one word with the first syllable of the next. Using the previous sentence we get – Seewha, Athap, Enswhe, Enyo, Utak, Ke-an, Anor, Rysen – you do the rest. Remember that while some of these won't sound cool, others will be just right.

► Search through books of myths and legends, preferably ones that are not well-known. They are treasure houses of great sounding names. Books of star names are useful too. Although here's me being old fashioned – try an Internet search. I Googled 'Star Names' and within moments I had Antila, Al Bali, Ancha, Tarazed, Althalimain, Sheratan, Prijipati, Tarf, Tegmine, Aludra, Procyon, Orlando Bloom – oops, wrong kind of star!

But what's in a name? Your readers will also need to be able to see what your characters look like. Let's move on young Modulehopper.

Picture a person★ ★

Using pictures in your head

Some people say that they can't create pictures in their minds and find colours impossible to imagine. My opinion about this is that everyone can learn to do visual stuff in their heads. Notice how the word 'imagination' is similar to 'image', which is a picture. If you meet someone who tells you that he or she 'can't do pictures', ask them if they remember their dreams. If they do, what do they remember? Sounds, smells, textures – or images? I believe that because our brains take in so much visual information, with a little practice everyone can visualize.

Ways to picture a person

Maybe you can already do it very well, in which case this technique will be easy. If you do find you have difficulty, get a 'picture partner' to help you.

The idea is to create an impression of what a character will look like in your story. In your imagination you can have all kinds of tools to help you – movie cameras, magnifying lenses, computers – just whatever you need. There are various ways of picturing a person:

► Imagine the whole person in the best way you can. How well can you see him or her? If not that well, pretend their image is on a computer screen where you can turn up the colours and the contrast. See how that works. What do you notice as you imagine your character in this way?

Tip: It's worth having a notepad and pen/pencil handy to jot down your ideas as they come to you. Even brilliant ideas can easily be forgotten.

► Look at your character through a movie camera. Do a slow close-up shot of the head and face. New details become visible. What do you notice? Now move the camera slowly downwards so that you can be aware of details of your character's clothes, hands, etc. Little details are important: a few such details woven into your story will help your character to come alive.

► Now get your character to turn around as you zoom out slowly to see the whole body again. Get your character to walk along and track him/her with the camera.

Module 25

▶ Your character meets someone (imagine this person too if you like). They talk. What does your character's voice sound like? Notice loudness (volume), pitch (high or low), pace (fast or slow), tone (soft or rough), emotion (mood).

▶ Now pretend you're standing there with your character. Touch his/her clothing. What does it feel like? Is your character wearing cologne or perfume? What does that smell like? What does your character have in his/her pockets? Ask and find out. Whatever you discover, remember that if you choose to use it there must be a good reason for that. Check back to **Ideas for a reason** (**Module 54**) if you're unsure about this.

Tip: If you work with a partner (s)he can go through these techniques with you. All you have to do is say what you're noticing. Your partner can jot down your impressions or just record your ideas on a laptop, tape recorder, etc. (can you still get those?).

▶ A powerful act of imagination is to pretend that you *are* the character. We came across this technique before, but now armed with all these other details you might find it's even more effective.

Something I often do when I've spent time with an imagined character is to thank him or her for being patient. Sounds crazy? I think that when you're serious about writing the first sign of a good imagination is talking to yourself. And the second sign is when you listen to yourself.

We'll come across **Visualizations** again in **Module 20**, but for now you may want to browse through some other character creation activities.

A bagful of games

Favourite room★

Draw or write about what a character's favourite room might look like and why. By doing this after a thumbnail you can gain useful insights into that person. So my character Kevin Howells (sticky-out hair and a wild look in his eye) has a bedroom that is quite untidy but he knows where everything is. He has a table by the window that's covered in books and papers – the table, not the window. These are mainly about science because that's his favourite subject, especially astronomy. Kevin's walls are covered with space posters – the Solar System, a shuttle launch, the constellations and suchlike. There's nothing about sport to be seen because he *hates* sport. He's got a small bookcase at the foot of his bed (which is to the left of his table). There you'll find Science Fiction books, super hero comics and a few fossils that Kevin found on a visit to the coast last year. He likes to sit at his table and gaze out over the back garden. A lot of the time he does this he's actually daydreaming, mainly about being an astronaut but sometimes about girls. He'd like to have a girlfriend but nothing too serious. He doesn't know it, but at school there's this one girl who really likes him but is too shy to say. Her name is Jane Hallowell and she's . . . But why don't you make up the rest yourself?

If-then-because★ ★

To play this game you need to know your character fairly well. You can either be your character (as in some of the games above) or speak for him/her. Work with a partner, who might prepare a list of 'if-thens' beforehand.

The idea is that your partner could say something like – 'If your character found a wallet stuffed with money lying in the street then he would . . .?' And you might answer 'Take it to the police station. Because his Mum lost her wallet once and nobody ever handed it in. It had her wages in and the family was really short of cash for a whole week!'

The purpose of the game is to explore reasons why your character would act as he or she does. You will not only learn more about the character's reasons and motives for things, but also make links between them to create a richer and deeper idea of your character's personality.

Tip: Now that you know how the game works, you and your friends might want to think of lots of 'if-thens', put them in an envelope and draw them out at random while one of you answers for their character. You can also build on any if-then in the following way:

> Your Friend: If your character found a wallet stuffed with money lying in the street then he would . . .?

> You (answering for character): Take it to the police station. Because his Mum lost her wallet once and nobody ever handed it in. It had her wages in and the family was really short of cash for a whole week!

> Friend: But if there was no photograph or address or anything except money inside, then . . .?

> You: He would probably keep it because Dad walked out last year and Mum still struggles to pay the bills . . .

In other words, play with each if-then situation to test your character's reactions.

Matchbox characters★ ★ ★

This is an easy game to set up but it takes some time to do. Also you may want to spend quite a long time discussing your ideas.

Find a matchbox or other small container. Your challenge is to collect as many small objects as you can that will fit into the box. Each object reveals something about your character – their personality, lifestyle, friends, etc. A fun variation is to get some friends to each make up a matchbox collection, then swap them with each other. Write a brief description of what you think the objects say about the character they refer to. If all of you write a description for every character, you'll find it interesting to compare ideas and opinions.

Another way of developing the game is to use a shoebox instead of a matchbox. This means – obviously – that you can collect more and/or larger objects. I visited one school where every pupil in one class made up a shoebox collection. From time to time a pupil would add something else to his box as a way of learning more about the character they'd invented.

Character ticklist★ ★

Getting facts about a character

This is simply a quick-check record that includes lots of facts about a character. You can make up a ticklist before you give more thought to what your character is like and then use it to build up a profile. Or, if you have already learned lots, it's a way of keeping these details in mind and to have them available to you at a glance. It's also true that when you write long stories or a series of short stories that use the same characters, you get to know these people over time. *Writing about a character helps you to learn more about that character* – in which case you can fill out a ticklist as you go along.

You can organise your list to suit your needs. I've suggested a possible format below (Figure 23), but please change it in any way you like. If you are 'scouting round' to find ideas and inspiration for characters, here are a few further tips:

▶ Notice people – and notice in different ways. As you look at a person what general impression do you get? Do you like the look of that person or not? Do they make you smile, chuckle, frown, feel annoyed? Think about why. Also notice little details about that person, like a particular piece of jewellery or the way they wear their hair. Sometimes a character description that links a brief overall view with a small vivid detail is all you need . . . *Bryant was a short but*

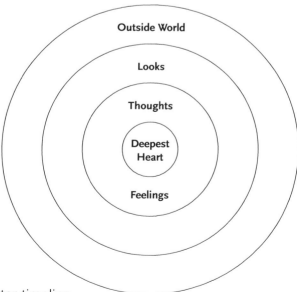

Figure 23 Character timeline

powerful-looking man. He had a gold tooth that glinted whenever he smiled/ Kenzie, tall, thin and pale faced, always had a knowing little glint in her eye that seemed to say 'I can see right into your mind' . . .

Tip: It's fine to be observant like this, but remember it's rude to stare (so use care!).

▶ Time hop. When you've observed someone that interests you imagine what that person was like when younger, or how they might look in the future.

▶ Ripple out. Use your imagination in the same kind of way to think about where that person lives, what friends they have, what they like to read and watch on TV, etc.

▶ Listen to people's voices. Notice the speed, pitch, volume and tone. If you hear part of a conversation, imagine what the rest of it might be like – if you're really keen you can even write down what you think. If you hear a snippet of conversation but can't see the people involved, this is a great opportunity to imagine what they look like. Jot your thoughts down. If you get a chance, compare your imagined character with what the owners of the voices actually look like.

▶ Observe one detail from each of ten different people and put them together to create a 'combo character'. You can develop this game by writing small observational details down on separate scraps of paper. Carry on doing this (even just a few each day is fine) until you have a big collection of scraps. You can then either put them all in a big envelope and draw some out to make a combo character, or you might be very organised and have one envelope for hair, one for noses, one for body shape and so on. By doing this you create a resource that will always be useful.

▶ When you go to the shops, take time to notice things that you would never buy in a million years – books, DVDs, clothes, food. Imagine what kind of people would buy them. Use those thoughts as a basis for inventing new characters. Note: You are not judging people in this activity. If you would never wear a bright pink shell suit don't be critical of someone who would (if you already own such clothing – good for you! Be your own person).

▶ When you read stories notice how the authors create their characters. If a particular character really stands out in your mind, think about how the author has achieved that.

▶ Think about someone you know and make six changes to that person's appearance/lifestyle/personality. Notice how they 'morph' into a different character in your mind.

▶ Listen to a piece of instrumental music and ask yourself 'If this music were a person, what would they look like, sound like, behave like?' and so on. You may be surprised and even amazed at how well your mind can do this!

Personality profile ★ ★ ★

Layered characters

Authors need to have a sense of their characters 'in the round', which is a very bad lead-in to the idea you'll find in Figure 23 the Personality Profile. It was the writer Alan Garner who said that people are like onions because they have layers (and, I add, they make you cry sometimes). The way the personality profile is set out uses this idea. If you decide to try it out then drawing/writing on a BIG sheet of paper will work best.

In the circle marked *Outside World* include thoughts, ideas and observations about a character's environment – the kind of home they live in, the neighbourhood, notes about networks of friends and so on. *Looks* obviously includes the way a character dresses but also gives information about body posture, facial expression, the way they walk and other things of that sort.

Thoughts and Feelings begins to explore the character's inner world or personality. What are their ambitions, fears, desires, likes and dislikes, etc.? *Deepest Heart* would include your character's most closely guarded thoughts and feelings. These might be things that even the character himself does not realise, but which would nevertheless influence their behaviour. (Remember that as an author you need to know more about your characters than you put in the story!)

If you like the circles idea then play around with it, change it to suit yourself. One young writer I met decided to draw a line bisecting the circles, so creating what he called a 'good side' and a 'dark side' to his character. Another writer in school cut out pictures to paste into the circles and even stuck on real objects to make a 3D collage of that character's personality. A group of pupils laid their big sheet of paper on a tabletop and placed objects relating to their character's life in the appropriate circles. As they talked about their character and learned more, things that started out as thoughts and feelings 'migrated' to the outer circles as they affected the character's appearance and the changing effect on his friends.

In other words – as with all of these activities – have fun as you learn to use them more and more effectively.

Hopefully now you've got a bunch of characters who fit well into the story you've been thinking about. Let them carry you on their shoulders like the hero you are to **Settings (Module 21)**.

Settings

Setting the scene

Many of the skills that we have previously touched upon find application here when pupils think about the settings for their stories. Some of the teaching of writing that I have come across in schools focuses solely on the mechanics of the craft while ignoring what might be called the 'organics of the art'. A major aim of this book has been to offer guidance in the development of the organics.

By this I mean in part allowing the flow of thinking and writing to happen without being troubled at that stage by technical accuracy. Of course technical accuracy is important ultimately to the clarity and power of the finished writing, but if a pupil's concern over where an apostrophe should go or whether to put 'where' or 'were' creates anxiety or interrupts the very creation of the sentence then that young writer's development is being hindered. If as an educator your ideology is that learning occurs by doing then the pupil's experience of forging language – of translating thoughts into meaningful words – lies at the heart of what goes on in the classroom. Having said that, experience is not just what happens but what one makes of what happens. If a pupil can reiterate your definition of a 'strong adjective' and remember the examples you've given but can't explain the idea in their own words or think of examples of their own, then their learning has been limited. The excitement of playing with words, crafting sentences, building narratives takes precedence at the creation stage. Afterwards comes reflection and analysis – though always with a light touch and a time limit built in. A review should never be an autopsy. Endlessly picking away at a piece of work to try and improve it finally falls victim to the law of diminishing returns. Experience arises out of new challenge. The late great Arthur C. Clarke maintained that in the end stories are never truly finished but only ever abandoned and this I believe is sound advice.

Experienced writers usually know when a sentence, paragraph or entire piece *feels* right (or wrong), even if sometimes they can't explain why. Or even if they can they aren't bothered about such explanations while the writing is happening. Howard Gardner's work suggests that we possess an innate capacity to make sense of the world through words. We glean meaning in the absence of any technical analysis of the language. Similarly I think we create meaning through words without necessarily being able to say in detail how we did it. I'm pretty sure I couldn't parse the sentences I'm using to explain myself now, though I feel I have a sense of their intended balance and tone.

This isn't meant to be an argument against the formal teaching of grammar. Hopefully what pupils learn in that way will connect with their 'organic appreciation' of language – their awareness of the effect of words combined with increasingly refined sensibilities so that what they draw from language and are able to build into their own writing becomes more powerful yet also more subtle and more diverse.

Simply put I think the most powerful creative writing occurs when writers are absorbed in reverie while reaching for the right words as they 'explain themselves to the world and explain the world to themselves'.

Useful classroom tips

Bringing all of this back to the point of the module (while bearing in mind that these ideas are more generally applicable), pupils may be encouraged to create vivid settings:

▶ By *writing sparingly*. A few details often stimulates the reader's imagination to work more than writing lengthy descriptions.

▶ By *remaining metacognitive* and entering the world of the story with all of your senses. *Be there*. What does the place look like, sound like, feel like, etc.?

▶ By *using vivid particularities*. These are details that combine a vivid sensory impression with an emotional response. Which of these do you think works better?

– The rain splattered against the window.

– The rain hit the window like handfuls of flung beads.

That is the essence of the vivid particularity.

▶ By *showing not telling*. In other words by creating a mental-emotional experience for the reader, which is more likely when the writer has had such an experience. Instead of writing 'Steve was frightened as he walked along the lonely street' think about how that street created the feeling of fear in the character. Once those details have been noticed, feed them back into the evocation of the setting.

Settings

Where is your story set?

Maybe you have already decided where you want your story to happen, which is great. But whether you have or not you might find these next few modules useful.

You know as well as I do that the setting of your story is important. In fact, it is one of the BIG THREE things to think about when you are making up your story – plot, characters and setting. Of course they are all connected. The setting influences what the characters say and do and helps to create the atmosphere or mood of the story. Just as you as an author must get to know your characters before you can do your best writing about them, so you must have visited the settings you want to put in your tales.

OK, OK – if you're writing a Science Fiction story set on Mars or a vampire story that takes place in the trackless forests of Transylvania you might not actually have been to those places (If you do go, please send me a postcard!). However it is vital that you go there in your imagination, because that's the only way you'll be able to take your reader there when he or she reads your finished story.

How to find your setting

▶ Remember what you learned in **All of your senses** (**Module 50**). When you imagine a place and then write about it, pretend you are *actually there*. Notice the sounds as well as the sights. What can you reach out and touch? What can you smell? How does that place make you feel? What do you notice that gives you the feeling? All of these little details can be useful, but remember you don't have to include every one of them in your work. In fact choosing just a few as part of your description of place often affects your reader's imagination more powerfully.

▶ Maybe some research would help. If you set a story in the Sahara desert then reading up on that place will help. And again you should look for vivid and interesting details. What colour is the Saharan sand? At midday, if you were standing there barefoot, how hot would the sand be? What creatures might you spot on your (probably painful) trek in search of an oasis? But wait a minute, do you find oases in the Sahara? Research can also help you to avoid mistakes of fact in your story. All right, so maybe a reader might not spot them, but if she does it could ruin her enjoyment of the tale . . . 'I was dragging myself across the hot Saharan sand crying "Water! Water . . ." when suddenly a polar bear lumbered over the dunes and bounded towards me!' See what I mean? I know I made a pretty obvious mistake there, but even small ones are to be avoided if you can help it. By the way, do polar bears 'bound'? And does the Sahara desert have dunes? The rule here is *if in doubt check it out*.

▶ Think back to **Ideas for a reason (Module 54)**. That point applies again now. Whatever you put in your story must be there for a good reason that helps to improve the story. It's especially useful to bear that in mind when you are writing SF, Fantasy or Horror because often the writer needs to work harder to make the story believable. The Science Fiction writer Douglas Hill once told me that he wanted to include a waterfall that went *upwards* on a planet he had created. But in the end he decided not to because there was no reason for it to be there. That's called professionalism.

Take it further

Anyway, that's enough to think about for now. If you are already happy with the ideas you have for your settings then drag yourself over to **Titles (Module 17)** (watch out for polar bears). Or:

▶ If you want some more practice in imagining a place breakdance across to **Visualizations (Module 20)**.

▶ If you fancy a bit of drawing trace a path to **Map making (Module 19)**.

▶ If you want to learn more about place names hokey-cokey on down to **Module 18** called – guess what? – **Place names**.

Visualizations

Multi-sensory thinking

In my opinion visualization is multi-sensory thinking by another name. The visual sense predominates in some people's imagination (while others say they 'can't do' pictures and colours) and this is reflected in the notion of the 'mind's eye' as opposed to the mind's ear, nose or fingertips. However, my belief is that 'sensory dominance' in the way we think is a habit of thought and that imagining with all of the senses is a skill that can be developed in everyone.

Being able to visualize and to be aware of what one visualizes is a function of metacognitive ability. This is what distinguishes what I call systematic daydreaming from idle daydreaming or being lost in reverie. 'Idle' daydreams (in the sense that we are not consciously active in their creation, content or flow) tend to drift from one to another by a process of loose association. Later, when we come out of the daydream we remember little of the content and all too often that also fades and the experience is lost. Systematic daydreaming on the other hand is daydreaming with intent. We consciously decide on the theme or topic of our thoughts and balance the subconscious drift of associations with conscious modification of those ideas to further suit our purposes. We can also deliberately focus on particular aspects of the imagined scenario and glean further information in so doing. Note that systematic daydreaming is not about trying to force ideas into being: conscious effort actually inhibits the 'organic' nature of the process. Yet at the same time the daydreamer is not entirely consciously passive, so that if for example I'm daydreaming about a street I want to describe as part of the setting of a story, I can choose to stop and look in more detail at particular features: I can enter one of the buildings and explore inside: I can switch day into night, and so on. Having made a decision of that kind, 'I' then sit back and notice what happens. That for me is the essence and skill of visualization.

Understanding pupil's visualizations

Any time spent helping pupils to learn to visualize is educationally valuable. While pupils visualize they are:

► developing metacognitive skills;

► learning how to internalise their attention;

► becoming more 'fluent' in multisensory thinking;

► increasing their ability to focus their attention (i.e. to concentrate).

Another aspect of pupils' ability to visualize concerns the scale or degree of detail of the thoughts they are able to generate. I have met pupils who can do 'overview thinking' brilliantly. In other words they can explain what their story will be about in a sentence but find it difficult to focus their minds on small-scale details of the plot. Such a pupil might easily conceptualise the hero as a young, handsome, brave adventurer but could not tell you anything further about that character's appearance . . . Or to be precise could not visualize anything further. The pupil might say 'He has dark blue eyes' but that would be as it were an abstraction or 'intellectual statement' rather than an idea based on the pupil having seen the hero's blue eyes in her imagination.

Conversely, other pupils are able to imagine in detail but find it hard to create 'big chunk' statements that reflect a narrative overview. Such an overview, supplied by you or the pupil, would again be an abstract idea. To talk about a Martian invasion of Earth or bitter rivalry between two families that spans generations would mean little if the pupil can't connect those big ideas to particular imagined details or places, people and events.

So in teaching pupils to visualize more effectively, notice needs to be taken both of the multi-sensory aspect of imagined worlds and the varying degrees of scale and detail by which they are created.

The filmic eye technique

One technique that can help in this way is the Filmic Eye – Figure 24. This activity works best if pupils have already had experience of 'stepping into' a picture stimulus and exploring it in a multi-sensory way. The Filmic Eye technique extends the process by encouraging pupils to imagine that they are not just the writer but also the director and principal camera operator in the movie of which the picture is just one scene. Use the vocabulary of film making as appropriate. A simple exercise would be to ask pupils to imagine they are filming the anxious-looking man in the picture as he walks down the street.

▶ Check multi-sensory thinking. Ask about the colours of his clothes for instance. Suggest that the pupils know what is in the small bag he is carrying. What sound does that make? What do they notice about the pace of his footsteps? How does the street smell (prepare yourself for poo references)?

▶ Check empathy. Ask the pupils to be that character briefly. How does he feel? What do his clothes feel like on his body? Describe his breathing, his heart rate.

▶ Check mental flexibility. In-role as the hurrying man, ask pupils what he is seeing as he looks to his left. If he were to stare straight ahead, what does he notice farther down the street?

BCU	Big close up	Mix	Blend one picture into another
Cut	Change from one scene to another	Pan	Moving panoramically up / down or sideways
Fade	Turning up or down sound / picture	POV	Point of view
Long Shot	View showing the whole scene	Zoom	Drawing away or closer-in

Figure 24 Filmic eye

Now get the pupils to be themselves again filming the hurrying man. Suggest that as they look through the camera they do a slow big close-up on his face. This brings out more and more details. Encourage pupils to 'talk these out' as they come to mind, or at least to have a partner note them down.

Change camera shots. Have a camera positioned in a nearby building. Suggest that a panorama is visible. Pan through a wide arc and notice further details – buildings, people, objects of interest.

Extending the filmic eye technique

Note that such a filmic technique can be extended through time. If that picture is part of one scene of the movie, what scenes led up to it? What will subsequent scenes include? This activity creates a good opportunity to introduce or revisit storyboarding. Because these days many pupils are very visually literate they may be more easily able to talk about sequences, scenes and shots than chapters, paragraphs and sentences – though the 'chunking' skills are the same in both cases.

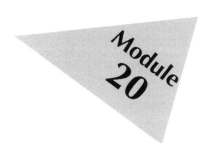

Visualizations

Learning to use your imagination

That word visualization means to imagine clearly – though not just to imagine what things look like in your mind but also what they sound like, feel like, smell like and even taste like.

Activities for improving your visualization

If you'd like to practise making your visualization stronger, have a go at these:

▶ Close your eyes and now describe the room as you remember it to a friend.

▶ Watch some scenes of a TV programme that's not familiar to you with the volume off. Imagine the character's voices. Think about their tone and mood, accent, loudness, pitch (deep or high). Now *listen* to some scenes of another programme with your eyes closed and imagine the characters' faces and body posture. Note – it doesn't matter if what you think doesn't match what's on the programme. The point of the activity is to practise using your imagination and to notice your own ideas.

▶ Think about a journey that's very familiar to you (a walk works best). Describe the route in as much detail as you can. Pretend you're a tour guide and point out places and objects of interest.

▶ Remember a meal that you really enjoyed. Take some time to eat that meal again in your imagination. Notice what it felt like to cut the food. Notice the colours if the food. What did the different ingredients of the meal feel like as you chewed? Describe what you tasted to a partner – but pretend that he or she has never tasted any of that food before. How will you get your friend to imagine the tastes that you remember?

▶ Imagine a dull rainy day. You are standing outside without a coat. You are cold, wet and shivering. Feel the rain. Listen to the gusting wind. Hear the splash and patter of the rain on the ground. Feel the bitter blast of the wind around your head and on your body. You tuck your hands tightly up under your armpits and hunch your shoulders. A really strong gust lashes at your eyes . . . If you shivered you have used your imagination really well.

Your teacher can show you other ways of boosting your powers of visualization, or you may want to hurry out of the rain to **Map making (Module 19)** or **Place names (Module 18)**.

Module 19

Map making

Mapping a story

Encouraging pupils to draw maps of where their stories are set helps them to visualize and otherwise organise their ideas. Begin perhaps by showing examples from literature, such as Tolkien's maps of Middle Earth (the Fantasy genre has an especially rich tradition of this). Notice place names and the settings they suggest. Help pupils to picture precise locations in their mind. What for instance would Ravenhill look like? Have pupils 'step into the map' and practise the multi-sensory thinking they have met elsewhere. The more pupils do this the more easily and vividly they will be able to create richly imagined scenes full of detail. If pupils are unfamiliar with the story to which a map refers, talk with them about what might happen there plotwise. Use this as an opportunity to remind them of some components that make for exciting stories – an ambush, a time limit ('Quick! We've got five minutes to reach the cave entrance!'), characters separating, entering unknown areas, a betrayal and so on.

Practise further by looking at maps of real places. Ordnance Survey maps are great for this. Familiarise pupils with standard map symbols and point out that these can be used as a kind of shorthand when pupils draw maps of their own. Compare map locations with aerial photographs of those same places. Suggest also that pupils use the Internet to research the kinds of locations they might want to use in their stories (thus building in educationally useful links to ICT and Geography).

Tip: Further ideas for using maps in this way can be found in *Jumpstart! Creativity* (under SatNav).

If pupils want to set their stories in an ordinary town or city you can suggest they start with a template blank such as that below (Figure 25). Ask them to decide on the kinds of locations that will feature in their story; a park, some wasteland, the inevitable haunted house . . . Help them to choose street and place names that are not only appropriate but which contribute to the genre and mood of the tale. Perusing street maps of towns and cities can throw up some lovely examples. For instance, while researching a Fantasy story I found on a map of Medieval Leicester *Dead Lane, Torchmere, Hangman Lane, The Skeyth, Hocx Bones* and, elsewhere,

Module
19

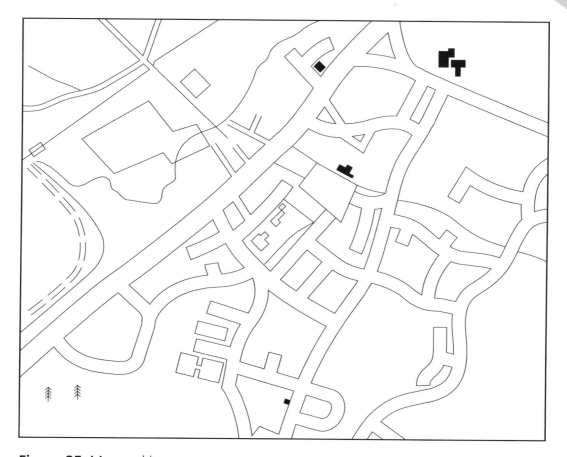

Figure 25 Map making

Tinkertank Alley which had such a delightful onomatopoeic quality I couldn't resist using it. Pupils can modify the templates just as they wish and, if they are glued onto a large sheet of paper – the templates, not the pupils – more extensive and diverse settings can be created.

Module 19

Map making

Draw a map

I don't know about you, but sometimes when I'm thinking up a story I love to draw a map of where it's set. Not only is this fun anyway, but I often have more ideas for my story when I'm drawing. Drawing and decorating your maps is not a waste of time. If you decide you want to do it here are some tips:

▶ Roughly sketch your map first in pencil so that mistakes and changes-of-mind can easily be erased. When you're happy with the map, ink and colour to your heart's content.

▶ Don't struggle to make up place names. Look at maps of real places. You can also get dictionaries of place names and these will give you some great ideas. Learn more about this in **Place names** (**Module 18**). Your teacher can also offer useful advice with your map-making.

▶ Look at photographs of the kinds of places you want to feature on your map and in your story. If you set a scene in a forest for example, research pictures until you find one that's just right for you.

▶ Another idea that might help you is what I call a 'combo town'. This is a place you invent that's made from bits of other places. For instance, I set quite a lot of my stories in a town called Kenniston. It contains some real locations based on places I actually know – a disused railway line (with a really creepy tunnel), a shopping mall that looks just like the one where I live, a park criss-crossed by avenues of trees, a corner shop that stays open late . . . But there are also parts of Kenniston I have invented or that belong to other places far away – lime pools (old lime pits that have filled up with water), a woodland covering a hill, a high 'ridge road' that gives wonderful views across the valley. In other words I have made Kenniston to suit what I want in my stories. And I can add features to it as well, as more story ideas come to mind. Another advantage of using a combo town like this in a number of stories is that you visit it often in your imagination so that, after a while, it seems as real as any actual place you know.

Take it further

As I said above, speak with your teacher if you need more advice. Or if you prefer hurry along the creepy tunnel down that disused railway line to **Place names** (**Module 18**) or hop-skip-jump to **Titles** (**Module 17**).

Module 18

Place names

Encourage browsing

Carefully chosen place names add detail and also texture and mood to a story. Encourage pupils to browse dictionaries of place names. There are many good dictionaries of place names available, one of the best I've found being the *Concise Oxford Dictionary of English Place Names*, though some pupils might find it tough going. Browsing such a rich resource however can make for a rewarding and enjoyable experience: pupils are usually interested in finding out what the name of their city, town or village actually means. In the process they pick up etymological snippets about place names in general. You can focus and extend such knowledge by showing the class some common elements of place names – bare, barrow, borough meaning grove or wood (or from a different root, hill or mound): beck meaning stream: clough meaning ravine or deep valley: ham meaning enclosure, and so on. Put up a list of such elements and encourage pupils to add prefixes, suffixes, adjectives and verbs as they experiment their way towards names they can use:

> Oakbarrow, Winterborough, Steepclough, Clough Deeps, Greenburn, Rickety Bridge, Tumblebrook, Lost Creech, Darkdean, Far Fen, Redfleet, etc.

Useful classroom tips

Also consider the following:

▶ Explore matching place names with the mood or tone of the story. Darkdean suggests a thriller or even Horror tale as it has a somber quality I think. Tumblebrook would make an appropriate location for an exciting and cheerful Animal adventure. Lost Creech could easily form the setting for a ghost story ('This place looks evil and dangerous. Let's split up and investigate!').

▶ Allow pupils to browse through road atlases. A brief skim might reveal such treasures as Zouch, Woodrising, Uyeasound, Upper Slaughter, Stonecrouch, Rumbling Bridge, Quarrywood, Odd Down and (the first place listed) A'Chill. Exploring street maps similarly leads to a useful harvest of names, though be prepared for the occasional potentially embarrassing episode as pupils discover Jeffries Passage, Brown Willy, Pratts Bottom, Crapstone, Balls Cross and Feltham Close. Note: these don't even make the top ten of risqué names in *Rude Britain* by Rob Bailey and Ed Hurst.

(Please note there are no **Teacher's notes** for **Modules 17–15**.)

Module
18

Place names

Useful tips for naming places

Knowing the names of countries, towns, streets and other locations adds detail and realism to your stories. Your teacher can give you more advice about this but here are some tips in the meantime:

▶ If you want names of places for a Science Fiction or Fantasy story (planets, magical realms, etc.) then search for star names on the Internet. Also browse through books of Astronomy. The same books of myths and legends you may have explored to find character names can also be useful now when you want names for your settings.

▶ For particular names of geographical features – forests, mountains and so on – work with your friends and speak with your teacher to make a list of 'landscape names' such as abyss, beck, bridge, chasm, crag, peak and others of that kind. Because you've thought about the genre of your story you're on your way to creating suitable names. So for an SF tale you might invent Fire Chasm, for a Horror story Haunted Crag would be good, for a Romance story Kiss-Me-Quick Lane is brilliant (no only joking).

▶ Look at atlases and street maps for useful names. Play around with what you find – mix and match names to see what new ones you can come up with.

Tip: If you don't know what a word means check it out. What for instance do these mean? – avenue, boulevard, close, crescent, cul-de-sac, mews?

Thinking about character and place names will often give you ideas for story titles too, but if you want some more help with that pucker up and walk down Kiss-Me-Quick Lane to **Titles (Module 17)**.

Titles

Writing a good title

The title of a story must:

1 Attract the reader's attention.

2 Interest the reader.

3 Tell the reader something about the story.

Have a look at some fiction books in the library. You'll see at once that the cover illustration, the style of the title's lettering (font, size, colour, etc.), the blurb on the back cover and even the words on the spine are designed to achieve at least the first two points in the list above. Of course, in the world of professional publishing books are not just trying to interest possible readers but also competing with each other. That's why the design team that helps to create the look of a book is so important.

As far as we're concerned what we want right now is an eye-catching title, but it's still worth thinking about what your story's cover would look like if it could ever be published. And if you have the time and opportunity and skill you might even want to design and draw that cover yourself.

What you'll notice about most story titles is that they're short and to the point, a bit like newspaper headlines. It's rare to find a title that's a full and complete sentence. Some titles amount to just a single word. Notice how a title might refer to a theme or a place, suggest a plot, name a character or important object in the story.

Activity

Suggestion: carry out a survey of fifty story titles to see how many fall into the above or other categories. And thinking about stories you like, how the titles might have helped to attract you to them in the first place. Here are some of my favourites:

▶ *The City and the Stars* by Arthur C. Clarke (adult fiction) – The title tells you at once that it's Science Fiction and it gave me that 'sense of wonder' about the universe which good SF can achieve.

Module
17

▶ *The Weirdstone of Brisingamen* by Alan Garner – What strange grandeur is in that title! What could a 'weirdstone' be? And who or what is 'Brisingamen'? This is obviously high Fantasy and part of the title's power is in its mystery.

▶ *The Giant Under the Snow* by John Gordon – The title suggests Fantasy (and the book's cover confirms it). I'm also told something about the season when the action takes place, and there's a sense of threat and menace there too. What kind of giant lies buried? And why? And what if it was dug up? See, I already want to know more!

▶ *The Haunting of Hill House* by Shirley Jackson (adult fiction) – This title is simple and straightforward and puts the story right there in the Horror genre. Notice the alliteration – the repeating of the H sound, which I think gives the title a 'whispery' quality like a soft but chilling midnight wind blowing through an opened window along dark and lonely corridors . . . Oh stop it, you're scaring me!

▶ *Galactic Warlord* by Douglas Hill – This tough, no-nonsense title speaks of conflict set among the stars; of space battles and exotic beings of the future. My much-missed friend Douglas Hill wrote four great stories about hero Keill Randor. This was the first and the others are *Deathwing Over Vaynaa*, *Day of the Starwind* and *Planet of the Warlord*. All four books were put together into one mighty volume called *The Last Legionary Quartet*. Notice again the alliteration of the L sound in 'Last Legionary' and also what a lot of work those two words do. They suggest huge military forces, desperate struggles and tragic defeats, while 'Quartet' lets you know what good value you're getting for your money!

These are some of my personal favourite stories and of course any list that you make will be different. But it is worth doing what I've done above, which is to wonder how and why a good title has an effect on you. With all of that said, you might want to make up a few titles of your own now – in which case hop into your starship and zoom over to **Word grid (Module 16)** or **Mix and match (Module 15)**.

Module 16

Word grid

Using the word grid

This technique works best if you have already given some thought to your story and have ideas about your characters, settings (including place names) and sequence of events. The idea is that you create a grid – I prefer using a 6 × 6 grid – and write a word that's connected to your story in each box.

To use the grid you can either simply scan the whole thing and wait for word-combos to jump out at you, or use a dice to choose words at random. If you decide to use a dice you'll need to roll it twice to reach a box. For the first roll count the number you get underneath the bottom row of the grid, then roll again and count upwards. In other words the dice rolls give you the co-ordinates of a word. Choose two words at a time and see if they suggest a title. Look at my example grid below, Figure 26, if you aren't sure how the activity works. These words by the way were taken from a Fantasy story I wrote; a trilogy called *The Wintering*. The three books are *Ice, Storm* and *Thaw* and it's about the boy Kell's adventures in a far-future ice age. You might want to experiment with my word grid before making one of your own. Below you will find some of the ideas that I had.

Tip: When this technique works well you can get more than one good idea for a title. In this case you'll need to think again about what a strong title aims to do and make a decision that way. The other titles or word-combos might even give you more ideas for new stories!

Some of my thoughts were – World Beyond the Shore, Shore World, Moon Beyond the Mountain, FrostWorld, Freemen of the Rim, Journey to Thule, Wulfen Sister, Rim of Heaven, Goddess of the High Places, Ice Goddess, Ice Wolf (from 'Wulfen'), Broken Sky.

Now even if you don't think a title is very good, keep a note of it somewhere safe. From time to time (I prefer to do this when I've finished one story and before I start the next) look through your folder or notebook of thoughts and you might be amazed of what new ideas and inspirations you have then.

If you're still looking for a suitable title, bundle up warm and trudge over to **Mix and match (Module 15)**.

ice	Kell	enclave	world	beyond	mountains
community	All Mother	journey	Wulfen	High Places	Edgetown
freemen	traveller	shore	Goddess	sky	heaven
horizon	wilderness	Shamra	broken	place	sea
blizzard	folk	darkness	war	frost	snow
light	moon	distance	rim	sister	Thule

Figure 26
Word grid

Mix and match

Surprise yourself

Often when people *try* to think of ideas their thoughts struggle along in only one direction and it all seems like a long hard slog. If you played with the word grid in **Place names** (**Module 18**) however, you've probably realised that there's a better way to do it – by taking yourself by surprise. When you want to be creative your mind loves the unexpected. If you used the dice to choose words did you have the experience of an idea just 'popping into your head'? The thoughts I had – Ice Goddess, Broken Sky and the others – simply just appeared and I didn't have to try and make them up at all. This is because in the deeper levels of your mind (what some people call the subconscious part) information is arranged as a kind of spider-web, where everything is linked to everything else. Paying attention to words at random (in this case from the word grid) causes new links to be made or old connections to be remembered. Such a connection is an idea that appears 'out of the blue'.

Always remember that your mind is a wonderful and powerful tool and it will not let you down when you believe in yourself and have a clear sense of what you want to achieve.

Some activities to try

Anyway, back to titles. This module is called **Mix and match** although the word grid was one way of doing that too. Here are some other suggestions:

▶ Copy down the titles of twenty books. Cut them up so that you have one or two words on each scrap of paper. Put them in an envelope and draw them out at random to see what happens.

▶ Look at some story titles and remember your parts of speech. If you've forgotten stuff about nouns, adjectives, verbs, etc. ask your teacher to remind you. Look at the way titles are constructed in terms of their grammar. So, for example:

  – *The City and the Stars* – noun + noun
  – *The Weirdstone of Brisingamen* – noun + noun
  – *The Haunting of Hill House* – noun (a kind of noun-verb mix) + adjective + noun (or you might say that 'Hill House' is a noun phrase, but let's not get too complicated)
  – *Deathwing Over Vaynaa* – noun + preposition + noun.

What we can do now is to fit new words into those templates. If I look at the word grid again I get things like:

► The Moon and the Wilderness

► The Warmoon of Thule

► The Haunting of the All Mother

► Darkness Over Edgetown.

Another little trick is to look at words like 'weirdstone' and 'deathwing'. These are combo words, made by putting two smaller words together. If you know what genre you're writing in it's easy to think of words you might find there. Scribble some down and try making combos:

► Romance – Twotimer, Heartbreaker, Dategame.

► Fantasy – Warsister, Snowheaven, Iceworld.

► SF – Skyworld, Starcrystal, Moonwars.

► Animal Adventure – Foxtree, Doomriver, Lostwood.

You'll find, as I did, that some ideas work better than others do. But that's to be expected. One of the principles of creative thinking is that 'to have your best ideas you need to have lots of ideas'. Power in numbers.

► Skim through a TV listings magazine and see what jumps out at you. There's nothing wrong with changing the title of a programme or movie to suit a story you want to write. I spent a few minutes browsing and came up with these:

The Day Before Yesterday (and also The Day Before Tomorrow – clever that one, I thought)/Him, Her and Me/Envy and Lovesickness/The Longest Night/From Daybreak Till Sunset/Claw and Disorder/All New You've Been Blamed/Northsiders/Storm Makers.

Once you get into the swing of this you may well find that ideas just tumble out on to the page. Not only might you hit upon a title that's just right for your current story, but also you'll have a treasure hoard of ideas for stories you can think about in the future.

You've done a lot of great thinking so far in this book and probably written plenty of notes. We're nearing the end of our countdown now and there aren't many more things to mention as you get ready to write. So let's move on to the last section – go to page 150.

Getting ready to write

Part 1

General guidance

These modules give pupils some guidance about narrative structure with an emphasis on the manipulation of time within the story. Inexperienced writers tend usually to think of narrative in a simple linear way. This 'mind set' is reinforced by the lesson that stories have a beginning, a middle and an end, which is perfectly true of course but can create at least two problems:

1   At the outset, when pupils are doing their first thinking, they sometimes don't realise it's fine to have an idea about the end or the middle of the story first. While we (rightly) encourage pupils to make sure their stories have a 'strong start' it can result in an overemphasis on the beginning with a corresponding lack of creative energy later on. Pupils sometimes 'run out of ideas' because they believe they can't think of anything else to say, they become bored and dispirited and quite frequently abandon the project.

2   The beginning-middle-end template often becomes a habit of thought over time, locking pupils' thinking into a restrictive linear way of envisaging story. This manifests itself in what I call the 'and-then syndrome'. The syndrome can be recognised by the following characteristics in the pupil's writing:

►   Simple linear B-M-E narrative structure.

►   Little or no manipulation of time in the form of flashbacks or other 'chronological jumps' (for example 'A year went by . . .' or 'Three weeks later . . .').

►   Often a corresponding lack of movement in space. By that I mean the writer's (and subsequently the reader's) attention stays with one character throughout, even if the story is written in the third person.

►   A noticeable lack of creative energy later in the story. This shows itself in various ways, such as the pupil actually repeating 'and then' often sometimes coupled with an abrupt and unsatisfactory conclusion. One also finds less zest in the writing coupled with little innovation: the plot limps along and one can imagine the writer struggling and wanting only to fill the required space on the page.

More confident and experienced writers don't worry about confusion. This is an interesting word because while it's usually interpreted according to its Latin root, to confound or throw into disorder, it can also be considered as con+fusion and read as 'flowing towards fusion' as in the confluence of two or more streams. The streaming of ideas from the subconscious level builds inexorably towards a plot that makes conscious logical sense.

This I feel is a vitally important point educationally. Many studies on how children learn reveal that when youngsters feel comfortable in the presence of ambiguity and uncertainty they learn more effectively. This is because they are not trying to 'guess the right answer' (as Edward de Bono might say) and, indeed, accept that there may be many possible answers. Such young learners also show a greater willingness to explore various alternatives and possibilities and are often more tolerant of other people's ideas, suggestions, theories and conclusions. For our purposes, pupils who exhibit this behaviour are likely to be more flexible and patient in their thinking as the story evolves 'organically' in their minds. They realise that the story is 'in there somewhere'★ and that developing a narrative is not about trying hard to work it out but relishing the joy of discovering that actually they know more than they thought they new.

Note: Many teachers I've met worry greatly that pupils need to produce writing of a desired level during SATs and often exhort pupils to 'hurry up and get it down on paper'. My belief is that when pupils feel capable and confident and have a range of thinking strategies available to them their 'thinking time' even under test conditions can be done quickly and effectively, and this will be reflected in the quality of their writing. The aim of all of the modules in this book is to elevate young writers to that degree of competence: the following batch of modules focuses particularly on time within narrative structure.

★ I've met many people, children and adults, who feel that they've got a book inside them somewhere, 'but if only I could get it out'. I'm reminded of an anecdote where, I think it was Benjamin Disraeli fell into conversation with a rather tedious wannabe writer at a dinner party. The aspiring author, seeking to impress, announced that she had a book inside her, to which Disraeli dryly remarked that that was probably the best place for it.

Module 14

Timespan

Inside and outside

Imagine that we've got our world (the 'outside world') and the world inside the story you are writing. The amount of time that passes inside the story from the beginning to the end is called the story's timespan. This doesn't have anything to do with the length of the story or how long it will take you to write it.

When people are learning to write stories they sometimes pay little attention to the story's timespan. Also in such stories time always moves along at the same rate – although this is more to do with the pace of the story rather than the timespan. (You can find more information about **Pace** in **Module 13**.) Having said that you might already have thought about the timespan of your tale. How much time passes from the beginning to the end? Does the whole story happen in a day? Or a week? Perhaps it's the other way round and all the events in your story take place within a few minutes or an hour. It's up to you of course because you're the author, though to be a good author you must give at least some thought to this matter of timespan.

Getting your head around time

Remember we looked at **Narrative lines** in **Module 38**? You can use a similar idea to get your head around the passage of time in your tale. I once wrote a short Science Fiction story called *Awakening*. It starts 'For many thousands of years Earth's people had slept'. The next page goes into more detail about how people had gone into hibernation for centuries after a global war while the planet recovered. After that they intended to wake and get on with their lives. But the plan goes wrong and the computers controlling the hibernation chambers malfunctions. The sleepers don't wake for hundreds of thousands of years.

So the timespan of the first half of the story is hundreds of thousands of years. The second half takes place over just a few minutes. We focus on one man, Andros, as he wakens slowly, not realising that such a great length of time has passed. He thinks that everything is normal as he opens his eyes and sees blurred movements beyond the misted glass of his sleep chamber. But things have changed terribly. He thinks that his friends have woken before him and are coming to help him now – though he's in for a shock.

Module 14

How would you end that story if you'd written it? Think about it before looking at the ending I chose below:

> 'The lid of the cabinet was wrenched open. Andros had no time to scream as the rat dropped down on him. It was as big as a man, and it held a knife in its hand.'

If we used a line to show the timespan of the story it would look like this (Figure 27).

When I wrote about great spans of time in the first half of the story my language was quite vague and general. I used phrases such as:

▶ Earth's people had slept

▶ great wars had devastated the planet

▶ whole continents had been laid to waste

▶ global superpowers had battled

▶ civilisation's last resources.

Notice that I don't go into any detail here. It would be the same kind of thing as saying 'a week went by'. You might put a bit of detail into what happened during that week, but the main purpose is just to mention the passing of time so that you can get on with the story.

On the other hand, in the second part of my story I do mention details. It's as though, in the time machine of our imaginations, we have materialised in a definite place and so we can notice little things like:

▶ the hiss of air being pumped into the sleep chamber

▶ the opening of Andros's eyes

▶ glass being smashed

▶ the glint of the knife in the mutant rat's hands.

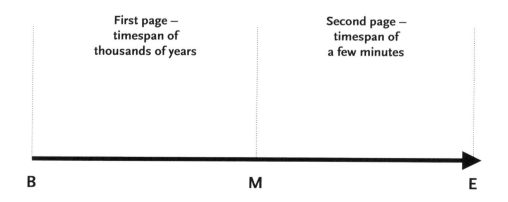

First page –
timespan of
thousands of years

Second page –
timespan of
a few minutes

B   M   E

Figure 27
Timespans

Module 14

This is a useful trick to learn. If you were writing a Romance story for example, and wanted to mention the early weeks of the characters' relationship you might describe things in general terms: the characters dating and falling in love, going on holiday, telling their friends, planning a future together. Then if you wanted to write a crucial scene where one character finds out that the other is let's say an international criminal, that scene, which may last only minutes, would contain more precise details.

Activities

Activity: Look again at a few stories you have really enjoyed and notice how the authors move the action on through time.

Activity: As you watch a movie or episode on TV, pay attention to the way the director lets you know that time is passing. We can learn a lot from these visual techniques and use them in our own writing.

If you want to find out more about *pacing* your story leap through the time portal and materialise at **Pace (Module 13)**.

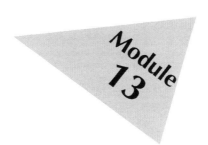

Pace

How fast do you go?

Pace means the speed or rate at which action happens and events pass by. Although many people like fast, pacy, action-packed stories the reader's enjoyment can be increased by varying the pace – or in other words deliberately slowing things down in between the action sequences. When the pace of a story is slowed it allows more descriptive details to be included and the characters can physically be sitting, walking, sleeping, etc. Or you can think of it the other way round, that by adding descriptive detail that slows the pace. Think about riding a horse. As the rider you sometimes want it to walk or trot and at other times to gallop. All you need is to have control of the reins.

How can you control pace?

So how can you make the horse gallop – how can you increase the pace of a story?

▶ Build in some action-packed incidents.

▶ Use shorter sentences and short paragraphs.

▶ Write brief scenes with frequent changes of scene and viewpoint. Several things happening at once can make a story zoom along, but you have to keep control of the action and be careful not to confuse your reader.

▶ Use strong powerful adjectives and punchy verbs (words ending in 'ing' also quicken the pace). Use adverbs that indicate speed and suddenness. 'Suddenly' is a good example.

▶ Use phrases that suggest speed – in no time at all/in the blink of an eye/all of a sudden/without warning . . .

▶ Include plenty of quick-fire dialogue, but balance dialogue (speech) with description. There is nothing worse than pages and pages of speech by itself – except pages and pages of description with no speech!

▶ 'Time jumping' lets the characters (and the reader) leap to where the action is. Writing something like 'The journey over the mountains took a week, but then the walls of the enemy city came into view' – means you don't have to slow things down by talking about the journey, unless things that happen on the journey are important.

Module 13

▶ Put in only the details that are absolutely necessary. When you've written the scenes, leave the work for a while then read it over again and take out anything that you think slows the pace.

Activities

If you want to practise these ideas, here are two activities.

1 Write a short fast scene about one of the following:

▶ A villain called Cutter drops a heavy flowerpot from a third-floor balcony in an attempt to murder Jo (or Joe, depending on what gender you want the victim to be). Our hero Chris (or Chris depending on what gender you want the hero to be) leaps forward and pushes Jo(e) out of the way just in time.

▶ The final few minutes of an exciting game of (pick a game of your choice, except chess) between opposing school teams.

▶ A car chase through city streets (or a dramatic landscape of your choice).

▶ Three people running away from a dangerous situation (pick a situation).

2 What can be done to make the following short scene 'pacier'? You might want either to suggest improvements or rewrite the scene to illustrate your ideas.

'It was night and the rain was coming down hard. Steve was cold and very wet. He had been trying to get away from the people who had been chasing him for over an hour but for some reason he had not been able either to hide from them or give them the slip, even though he had really, really tried. He was wearing dark sneakers, blue jeans (there was a patch on the left knee), a thin black windcheater (that's why he was so cold, because the material of the windcheater was thin and the cold wind went right it). He was not wearing a hat.

'Steve turned down an alley. He was trying quite hard to find either somewhere warm and dry, or at least somewhere where he could hide from the people who were after him. He wasn't sure why these people were chasing him, but maybe he thought it could have something to do with the wallet he'd found lying in the street that afternoon (the wallet was lying in the street, not him).

'Anyway, he turned into this alley and then gave a gasp as he saw someone up ahead. It was nothing more than a big dark shadow but Steve just knew (although he didn't know how he knew) that this person meant to do him some harm. "What do you want?" Steve said as he tried to keep the nervousness out of his voice. The figure jumped at him and they had a fight.'

I'm sure you spotted all kinds of ways of making the scene faster and more exciting. Here are some of the things I would do:

▶ Shorten that third sentence. It's too long and difficult to read. Maybe this would sound better – He had been running for an hour and was desperate to give his pursuers the slip.

▶ Get rid of the description of his clothes or mention them as part of the action. 'Suddenly he slipped, stumbled and tore his black windcheater.'

▶ Delete the sentence about the hat and maybe mention he was bareheaded earlier.

▶ I'd cut the second paragraph down a lot and leave out the pointless explanation that's in brackets. I'd say something like 'He knew why he was being followed – they wanted the wallet he'd found that afternoon. He hadn't even looked inside and wished now he'd just left it lying there in the gutter.'

▶ I'd have him turning into the alley in the third paragraph (leaving out the word 'anyway').

▶ Although dialogue can increase pace it's only Steve who speaks. So I think I'd simply have Steve saying 'Who are you?' but realising it was pointless to ask. Then he'd turn around to see a second figure blocking the other end of the alley. He was trapped.

▶ I'd make the figures approach him silently as he feels panic rising in him. He looks around for a weapon, any weapon. He thinks he doesn't have any choice but to fight for his life.

▶ I'd describe the fight! This is a great opportunity for some action and gives me as a writer a chance to practise different ways of creating a fast pace.

That's a little bit on pace. Now let's move on quickly to look at **Flashbacks** – jump to **Module 12**.

Module 12

Flashbacks

Backwards and forwards

Steve got up that morning and went to the bathroom to wash and shave. Then he got dressed, had his breakfast, put on his coat and stepped out of the house. He bought a newspaper from the corner shop and also a bar of chocolate, which he thought he'd eat on the way to work because he didn't bother to make himself breakfast. He stopped to look through the window of the DVD rental shop on the High Street and thought he might watch a movie after work that night. Then he took his usual route through the park. He had just reached the other side when a car with blacked-out windows screeched to a halt beside him. Two men scrambled out on to the pavement, grabbed him and bundled him back inside. The car shot away down the road even before the rear door was pulled closed.

A car with blacked-out windows screeched to a halt beside Steve as he walked along the street. Two men scrambled out on to the pavement, grabbed him and bundled him back inside. The car shot away down the road even before the rear door was pulled closed. But the morning had started normally enough . . .

Which story opening do you prefer? Why? I'm hoping you picked the second example because that's the one I think is better too. You know that a story must grab the reader's interest straight away. This is important enough in a long story like a novel, but it's absolutely essential in a short story where you can't afford to take a long time to get to the point.

Notice in the second example how we're right there in the middle of the action from the start. The paragraph ends by leading into a flashback – the next paragraph might say a bit about what happened to Steve earlier that morning, or some time in the past that was relevant to the story. It's a useful trick because it means you can 'hit the ground running' at the start of your story, develop the plot a little and then, if you need to, jump back in time to explain a bit about what led up to the crisis.

How does flashback work?

The word *flash*back gives us a clue about how the technique works. The jump back in time happens quickly and so takes just a few words – two months earlier/the previous night/over a century ago/less than an hour before, etc. is really all you need to introduce a flashback. It's easy to do, but you need to have thought about your story first and build it into the planning.

Using the flashback technique

Use flashbacks as a way of getting your story moving quickly. If you like using them you might want to have a go at something more ambitious:

▶ Introduce a crisis and then build up towards it through a few flashbacks. When you're back in the present, put in your resolution. So a guy could be facing the firing squad. He thinks back to the events that have put him in such a situation. He comes back to the present moment when he hears the click of the rifles preparing to fire. And then . . . ? Or a man asks a woman to marry him. Use flashbacks as she thinks of various occasions in her life when they've dated. Come back to the present moment. As he offers her the engagement ring she says . . . ?

▶ Start a story with a really dramatic situation involving three or four people. Tell their separate stories in the form of flashbacks that bring the reader up to date. How then does the dramatic situation resolve itself?

▶ A hero lies dying after a mighty battle. His mind wanders back to different events in his life. At the end of the story his eyes flicker open and he sees . . . ?

Let's flash forward now to **Story arcs (Module 11)**.

Story arcs

Weaving through the story

If you imagine a story as a simple line (as in Figure 27) then a 'story arc' is another line that loops away from it and comes back in at a different point (Figure 28a). Or it may be a kind of thread, focusing on one character, that weaves its way through several stories – but let's not get too complicated about it!

In the way that I'm using the idea, a story arc is linked to the notion of a *sub-plot*. This is a kind of story-inside-a-story. It can happen when characters split up for some reason, in which case the adventures of each of them would form a different sub-plot within the main story. All of these arcs would then loop back into the main story (perhaps not all at the same point) – Figure 28b. Story arcs are often used not only in books but in comic series and in TV series too – the very popular *Doctor Who* for example uses story arcs a lot, where we meet a minor character in one story who then becomes a key character in another story.

Useful tips

If you do feel confident and would like to make stories with arcs, here are a few ideas. The diagrams in Figure 28 give you a picture of how they would work:

▶ Figure 28a – a minor character is introduced then drops from the action. He rejoins the story later and talks about his adventures (perhaps in flashback).

▶ Figure 28b – Two characters are together for the start of the story, then split up. The bulk of the rest of the story is told as three separate sub-plots which follow their adventures until they meet back up towards the end.

▶ Figure 28c – An important object is lost, then found, then stolen, then rediscovered. Each of these events is marked by a star on the diagram.

▶ Figure 28d – Three characters begin a story together, then something dramatic happens which sends them away on separate adventures, each told as a different story.

I hope you've grown 'arcustomed' (bad pun) to the idea of story arcs. Let's learn a bit more using **Story paths (Module 10)**. Loop your way over there now!

Module
11

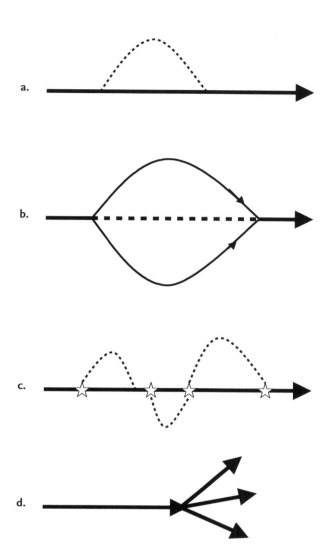

a.

b.

c.

d.

Figure 28 Story arcs

Story path

Choosing a path

A story path is a way of working out the events of your story scene by scene. You may already have done this by now of course, in which case perhaps you'll find the idea useful when you plan your next story!

A typical story path follows the narrative line you've thought about, but includes a number of 'notes-boxes' where you can write in more detail. See Figure 29. Note that I've made the narrative line a zigzag shape to fit it on the page – you can if you want to keep it as a straight line; if you do, draw it on a LARGE sheet of paper.

Ways to use a story path

A story path can be as simple or as complicated as you want it to be. If you like the idea, here are some different ways of using it:

▶ **Group work**. Story paths work well if you are planning or writing stories with your friends. You can all look at the sheet, see how far you've got and discuss what to put in the next scene. Then you note your ideas on a post-it or file card and place it along the path.

▶ **Storyboarding**. If you haven't looked at storyboards, ask your teacher about them now. Storyboards are sequences of drawings that help to plan a story visually. They were first developed in the 1930s by the Walt Disney studio (according to the online encyclopedia Wikipedia) and are still used a lot in the film and TV industry. My idea of a story path really grew out of thinking about how storyboards are used. If you love drawing then you can create a storyboard/path of your ideas and this will help you to turn it into words later.

▶ **Comic cut-outs**. Maybe you love comics, as I do. You can copy or cut out panels from comic books and stick them on to a story path to make a new story featuring your favourite heroes and villains.

▶ **Photo story**. These days with digital cameras taking photographs is easy. Work out a story with some friends (using a story path), then create it visually by taking and printing your pictures and sticking them to the story path. Add dialogue and short descriptive notes as necessary.

Module 10

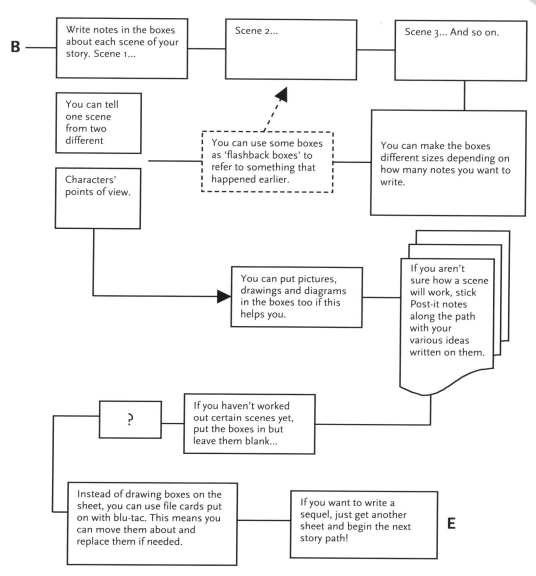

Figure 29
Story path

► **Board game**. If you've already got some ideas for a story you can easily turn it into a board game. All you need is a board game template – Figure 30 shows an example – dice and counters. In each square will be an instruction. It can be as simple as 'Gain 5 bravery points' or a writing task such as 'Describe your main character's ideal day'. The point of the game (apart from having fun!) is to help you to work out your story in more detail, to learn more about the characters, to invent new scenes, rehearse dialogue and so on.

By now you'll have done most of the big thinking needed in order to do write a great story. There are a few more bits and pieces to mention, although you may not need or want to look at them now. Check the flowchart at the start of this book to find out what the remaining modules are about, then pick the ones you want to visit.

Module
10

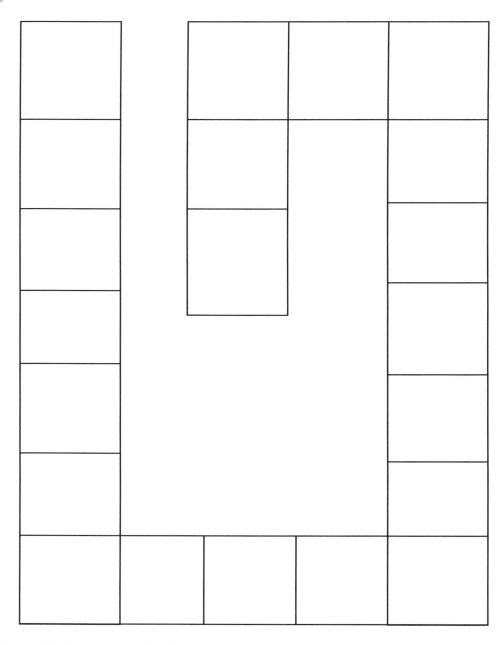

Figure 30 Board game blank

Getting ready to write
Part 2

One step at a time

An underpinning assumption of this book has been that when young writers have done their 'major thinking' with regard to the main structural components of a narrative they will be in a better position to concentrate on the smaller-scale details. An apt metaphor would be that when pupils have mapped out their route they are better able to notice and enjoy the scenery on the journey. I think that a huge barrier to the creation of effective writing and the enjoyment of the process is trying to do everything at once. In other words it's very difficult and not much fun to try and have ideas about a story as you try to frame them in meaningful language, as you try and write neatly and accurately. However, once the story has been broadly visualized and some 'meatier' notes made of key aspects of plot, setting and character then the flow of composition can occur and the story unfolds on page or screen more naturally. One's best writing I contend is effortless, because much of the assimilation has already been done. Details of the scene being written emerge in the mind (visually, auditorily, kinesthetically) and although there is to some extent an intellectual 'reaching' for the right words they seem to offer themselves up moment by moment accompanied by the feeling that 'yes, that's what I want to say'. This is indeed a creative flow in the same sense of the word that an accomplished musician's performance flows from her hands or an athlete's peak performance flows from his body. Body, mind and the tools of the trade are integrated and in such a state the writer (in our case) loses himself in the creative outpouring and often, upon stopping when the wave has crashed, comes back to himself in the here-and-now and thinks 'Wow, did I write that?'

A huge amount of research has been conducted into the relationship between creativity, physiology and brain states. Any good book on accelerated learning will explore this to some extent and a few such books are referenced in the Bibliography.

Creativity and physiology

The point I want to make from this is that the teaching of creative writing is not simply a matter of helping pupils to master the technicalities of the language but

Modules
9–4

also to cultivate in them the capacity to 'switch on' that creative flow and to have it serve the framing of ideas in words most powerfully and satisfyingly. By way of summary I think that as teachers we can best help pupils to become competent writers when:

▶ We recognise and communicate to pupils that thinking comes before writing, which comes before reviewing (i.e. refining the work and tidying up technical errors).

▶ We cultivate the belief that the mind is potentially an endless source of ideas. The American writer David Gerrold says that a creative writer is a 'perpetual notion machine', which hits the nail on the head.

▶ We instil in pupils an enjoyment of the process of writing and value the outcomes of their thinking. In other words we celebrate the achievements of writing above and beyond and before we are forced to benchmark their attainment.

This last point is crucial. I have made a distinction between achievement and attainment ever since, years ago now, I set a class some homework. I asked the pupils to sit quietly at home and to think about the story they were going to write later in class, and to make some notes about plot, character and setting. One boy, Ben, turned up next lesson with a grubby scrap of paper covered with virtually illegible scrawls and no punctuation. Perhaps he did not see the horrified look on his English teacher's face, because he was still smiling as he explained that, even though with several brothers and sisters and his Mum and stepfather quarrelling he had nowhere quiet to think, he had nevertheless spent over an hour on this work. I realised in that moment what he had achieved and I gave him a merit point on the spot.

▶ We teach by example. Do we display the same love of language and curiosity for words that we want the pupils to have? Despite a pressured curriculum and the ever-present threat of inspections and league tables, do we take time to read stories to the pupils for pure enjoyment (enjoyment being the most important 'learning outcome' that exists)? Do we as teachers ever sit and write as the pupils write? It's a salutary experience because it immediately allows us to appreciate the tribulations and the elations the pupils experience.

▶ Do we 'go beyond the given' and help pupils to become not just literate, but linguistically intelligent – helping them to fulfil the potential of using language as a life enhancing and life transforming tool?

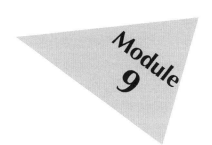

Length of story

Finding an ideal size

Truly speaking every story has its ideal size. In other words a story takes as long as it takes. Some stories 'naturally' take a page or two to tell and if they were made longer they'd feel thin or would appear padded. On the other hand to compress a story that really needs to be longer means leaving out necessary detail and rushing through events just to make it fit. The pace and balance of a well-written story take precedence over an artificially imposed length.

Having said that, learning to write to a predetermined brief is part of the writer's craft. Professional authors often have to follow publishers' guidelines, which sometimes includes making the work a certain length. For that reason alone there is value in cultivating the necessary control and discipline to 'write to order'. For our purposes it's also useful for pupils to have the necessary inventiveness and flexibility to assemble and express their ideas clearly within time constraints and length limits. Pupils who can think and plan effectively and write confidently are more likely to give of their best under test conditions for example.

Given then that pupils will be asked to write stories on particular topics, of a given length and within a certain time, it's important for them and us if we view it as part of the creative challenge of authorship. That means cultivating the attitude of relishing such a challenge while minimising the stress and anxiety that could so easily accompany the task. An environment of low stress and increased creative challenge is most conducive to pupils' high achievement.

Helping pupils to write to order

There are many ways of helping pupils to practise writing to order. Consider the following:

▶ Once a story is written, ask the pupil to look through it again with a view to adding scenes that would make it even better. Note that this doesn't necessarily mean actually writing the scenes out, simply deciding where they would go and what they would be about.

▶ Read through a story with the class and ask the pupils how they would make it shorter. Could any scenes be left out entirely? Could sentences be written more concisely?

Module 9

▶ Ask pupils to sum up their own or others' stories in a short paragraph. You could link this with a blurb-writing activity where a plot summary and reasons why it's a good read must fit on the back cover of a standard paperback.

▶ Practise writing minisagas. These are stories of exactly fifty words (plus up to ten words for a title). Typically first time around a pupil will write more than fifty words and must then chop out extraneous material and reword what's left. It's a great test of editorial skills. Here are a few minisagas to illustrate the point.

The Attempt. A sheer cliff face. He would jump. His head was filled with thoughts of nothing but failure and hopelessness. However, this time success meant everything. He leapt off the cliff . . . The green sea raced towards him – The baby bird flapped its wings and began flying for the very first time. By Sam Marsh.

The Worst Day at College. First day at college, full of loneliness and despair. I felt like half of me was missing. Half of me had faded away. I walked through the front door. Mum asked 'How was it?' I was upset. I can't believe Phil dumped me! I will never go to college again. By Ashleigh Harrison.

I Had to Live with My Mistakes. I watched him as he lay there in our bed. I had married him and I was still regretting it. I didn't want him. I wanted his brother. I heard tip toeing behind me. He put his arms around me. 'Come back to bed.' I had to live with this. By Rebecca Whitmore.

Module 9

Length of story

Choosing your story's length

When I was a kid at school and had to write a story I would always ask my teacher how long it had to be. What was in my mind was 'The shorter the story is the less effort I'll have to make and the less time it will take.' But that isn't the best attitude to have. The best attitude to have is 'What must I do to make my readers really enjoy my story?' I think that must lie at the heart of all good writing.

Some useful tips

Having said that, you will sometimes be asked to write quickly and to a certain length within a certain time limit. So what's the best way of doing it?

► First – don't panic. Give yourself time to think about and plan the story. Make some short notes. These will be handy reminders later on.

► Keep your writing clear, simple and to the point. Remember that your reader will fill in a lot of the details – that's what imaginations are for.

► Use fewer, shorter words instead of more and longer ones. Also shorter sentences usually work better than longer ones.

► Spelling and punctuation are important but don't worry about them while you write. Just tell your story. If you can't quite remember a spelling just write what you think is correct. If you're writing in pen, have a pencil with you too and anything you aren't sure about put it in pencil and go back later to think about it further.

► If you're in a test, give yourself some time at the end to go back and read through your work. If you want to change entire phrases or sentences, put a neat line through them and write the correction neatly nearby.

► Most importantly, enjoy writing the story. The more you enjoy it the better your story is likely to be and the more your reader is will enjoy it too.

Economy of language

Keep it simple

As I advise pupils in their notes on **Length of story** (**Module 9**), generally speaking shorter is better. Using fewer words, simpler words and less complex sentences generally makes for clearer communication. Effective writing is not just a matter of the extent of one's vocabulary but how the words are used. Two immediate issues arise from encouraging pupils to try to use what I call an 'inflated vocabulary', i.e. words they are not familiar and comfortable with:

▶ Parroting. This is simple feedback by pupils of individual words, phrases or other language patterns that an adult – often their teacher – has advised them to use. One common example occurs when we recommend that pupils use a variety of connectives. Ultimately this is good advice but can all too easily result in pupils' writing taking on an artificial, over-formal tone. The writer and educationalist Pie Corbett suggests that a useful strategy is 'imitate, innovate, invent'. If parroting is a temporary phase leading towards a more fluent and individual use of words then I feel that it is acceptable.

▶ The 'OCR Syndrome'. This is simply using words without understanding what they mean. I coined the term when I asked a class of primary pupils how they thought a story was constructed. I expected 'the beginning, the middle and the end' as a reply, allowing me to develop the idea from there. But instead the pupils said 'orientation, complication and resolution'. I asked them what those big words meant. One pupil shrugged and said 'I don't know, Miss told us.' I asked Miss what they meant and she began to look through her lesson plans . . .

This is perhaps an extreme example but relevant all the same. Sometimes parroting and the OCR Syndrome go together. I recall speaking with an AS Level English student about some work he'd done and he told me that he'd written it in a certain way because that 'impacted on the verisimilitude of the lexis'. I asked him what it meant, since I didn't have a clue. But neither did he. He had been advised to use certain terms in his commentary on the work and was simply repeating these back to me now.

All young writers display an emergent understanding in their use of language. Perhaps they may be forgiven for using it in the ways outlined above, but I do feel that it is so important to allow them to evolve as writers through a love of words rather than trying to 'force grow' their output simply to satisfy imposed levels of performance.

Module 8

Economy of language

Saving your words

The word economy means 'to manage'. Usually we link it with managing money but it's just as useful when we think about words. Economy of language isn't about writing as little as possible – i.e. 'saving' words – but *managing* them so that they do the best job they can. So how can we make that happen?

▶ When you're describing a character or scene there's no need to write everything you know. Put in a few clear details and let the reader's imagination do the work.

▶ You may have learned about compound and complex sentences, but when writing stories, shorter, simpler sentences usually work better.

▶ Never use words you don't understand. First, you might use them wrongly but also knowing what a word means enriches your thinking about it.

▶ Avoid lists of adjectives. Anything over three is cumbersome. You could get away with 'It was a cold, dark, rainy night in November' but not 'It was a cold, dark, rainy, windy, lonely, scary night in November' – at least, not unless you want to make your reader chuckle.

▶ Don't just tell your reader about things, give him an experience of them. Make him feel what the characters feel. If a character feels frightened, what is he seeing or hearing, etc. that makes him or her feel like that? Mention it to help your reader have that feeling too.

▶ Break up blocks of description (narrative prose) with speech, but make the dialogue work for you. The best dialogue tells us something about the character, adds to the atmosphere of the scene (scary, funny, etc.) and moves the action on.

▶ Well-chosen similes and metaphors can save you a lot of description. We use them all the time, in fact. Saying that somebody has 'rosy cheeks' means the colour of their cheeks is similar to the colour of rose petals. 'Rosy' does in one word what took me the rest of the sentence to repeat. Look back to **Metaphors (Module 49)** if you want to refresh your memory.

▶ When you read stories notice how other authors manage the language. You can pick up some great tips from other people – and don't worry, it isn't copying.

Connectives

Using connectives creatively

Using a variety of connectives is one surefire way of improving a pupil's test scores (parroting and the OCR Syndrome notwithstanding). However, while connectives tend to be lumped together grammatically, they require us to do quite radically different things within our imaginations. To understand the concept of *meanwhile* for example we need to make a spatial leap in our heads and be able to do 'big chunk' overview thinking . . . 'The car crashed through the fence and came to halt, teetering precariously on the cliff edge. Emily opened her eyes and let go of the steering wheel, hardly daring to breathe. Meanwhile back in the city Jeff listened to her voicemail message telling him she was going to visit her lawyer.' Visually it's a sudden change of scene. If the following sentence in our nail-biting story was 'Yet even as Jeff realised that Emily was leaving him, his thoughts drifted back to the summer before, when everything had seemed so perfect between them.' Now we need to make a temporal leap as well.

This is quite complex thinking – perhaps not to us because we are more experienced visualizers, but some pupils might struggle. What I am trying to highlight here is that a 'thinking agenda' and the formal teaching of connectives might go hand-in-hand. Then instead of being, at worst, dry grammar learned by rote, pupils can experience the mental effects of connectives and thereby gain a greater understanding of how they are used. Here are a few suggested activities to achieve that:

► Read out some sentences containing connectives and ask pupils what's going on in their heads. In other words encourage metacognition as you introduce and rehearse conjunctions and prepositions.

► Play games that highlight the function of certain connectives. For instance, play the *Meanwhile Game*. Think of a series of concentric circles with the starter sentence (the initial focus of attention) in the middle. 'Emily's car teetered on the cliff edge. Meanwhile in the city Jeff listened to her phone message. Meanwhile fifty miles away in another city Emily's lawyer was waiting for her to arrive. Meanwhile across the Atlantic in New York Jeff's new girlfriend . . .' Notice that with each 'meanwhile' our imaginations expand in space to create an ever-larger overview. You can play it the other way round also and start with some far-flung scene and 'step it in' progressively towards (in this case) Emily's precarious situation.

▶ Link the teaching of connectives with an activity like the Filmic Eye (see **Visualizations** (**Module 20**)), where a single visual resource can act as a focus for a number of connectives. Stick the picture on a board and create a 'connectives spidergram'.

▶ Bring the teaching of connectives into 3D space. Play the Meanwhile Game in the hall/playground and have pupils physically move out from a central point. Encourage the pupils to invent other movement games that literally 'embody' the concepts that lie behind connective words. For instance, create a character time line by putting a length of ribbon or string along the floor. Place objects along the line to represent particular events in that character's life. Other pupils start from now and play the *Before Game*, walking back down the line into the past. Then return to now and play the 'After Game' by speculating about the character's future.

Module 7

Connectives

Using connectives well

You've probably done some work on connectives with your teacher, in which case you'll know that these are words and phrases that link ideas together. I don't want to repeat things you may already have talked about, but perhaps these few tips can add to your writing toolkit:

▶ Don't use lots of different connectives just because you've been told to. Only use them (as you would with any other word) because of the job you want them to do. It's useful to have a connectives chart or mat in the classroom where you can see a choice of words. Think about the kind of link a connective makes before you use it.

▶ There a many different connective words and phrases and I don't suppose anybody expects you to know them all by heart. I have found that to learn and understand more of them it's handy to put them into groups. So for instance we can find:

- connectives that make links in time and space: earlier, meanwhile, next, then, after;

- connectives that act like little blobs of glue (I call them 'sticky links') and joins the cause of something with the effect it has: so, because, as a result of, therefore, caused;

- connectives that help you to make lists: first, second, etc., and, also, as well, another.

Extension activities

Anyway you get the idea. If you haven't already put connectives into groups like this have a word with your teacher who will be delighted to assist you.

▶ Thinking of some connectives as objects can help you to understand the job they do. I've already mentioned a word like 'because' reminds me of a blob of glue. 'Because' sticks a reason on to an idea. 'The cat slept all afternoon because she had eaten a bowlful of her food.' I think of 'and' as a hand that grabs hold of and joins up with the rest of the sentence. 'The cat slept all afternoon and through the evening and for most of the night.' 'But' reminds me of a closed gate that can stop me going along a certain path. 'Steve enjoys a lie-in at the weekend but would never stay in bed past ten a.m.' This trick works for some connectives but not others, though it's worth investigating.

► Play connective games where the same connective is used many times. This helps you to become familiar with the job it does and can give you ideas for new stories (and it's fun too!). For instance, try the 'this caused' game:

– Steve fell asleep on the couch.

– This caused him to miss his bus.

– This caused him to be late for the cinema.

– This caused the friend he was meeting to be very cross.

– This caused Steve's friend (Dave) to write him an angry email.

– This caused Steve to be angry in reply.

– This caused a break in their friendship.

– This caused Steve to go out and look for new friends . . .

Or have a go at the 'fortunately but unfortunately' game:

► Steve fell asleep on the couch.

► Unfortunately he didn't hear the smoke alarm.

► Fortunately his neighbour did.

► Unfortunately the neighbour didn't like Steve and failed to warn him.

► Fortunately Steve smelled smoke and woke up.

► Unfortunately the front door of his flat was jammed.

► Fortunately he could open the window.

► Unfortunately the flat was on the tenth floor . . .

Look for other connectives that you can turn into a similar game.

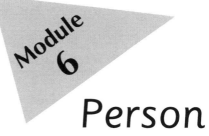

Person

Step mentally into the picture

Developing pupils' understanding of this aspect of grammar also requires the ability to visualize. Writing in the first person from a character's viewpoint necessitates seeing the world as that character would see it. This is not just about visualizing but also empathising; being able to 'resonate' emotionally with how a chosen character feels and reacts. One quick yet effective way of introducing this is to show the pupils a picture of a street scene and practise stepping mentally into the picture. Initially get them to imagine what the street looks like as it were through their own eyes. This in itself involves mental flexibility and a shift of perspective. Then step back out briefly. Explain that when they step in again the pupils must imagine that they jump into the body of, say, an old person who lives alone; or a cat burglar looking for a likely target; or even an animal such as a cat. What thoughts, feelings and sensations do they imagine looking at the world from that perspective?

First person

The value of first person writing is that it allows the author to explore a character very intimately. We can sift through his (or her or its) innermost thoughts and have that character talk directly to the reader. The downside of a first person perspective is that the author and readers must stay with that character constantly throughout the story.

Second person

The 'you' voice is used less frequently these days but has found great popularity in the choose-your-own adventure stories first popularised in the 1980s and now enjoying a new lease of life. Using this technique pulls the reader into the story and is immediately involving. 'You are walking down a dark corridor and can see only a short distance ahead of you. Unexpectedly you come to a T-junction. If you decide to turn left go to page X. If you choose to turn right go to page Y.' There are of course pitfalls and perils scattered throughout the narrative, including (in the CYOA books) the chance of being killed off – in which case you have to 'respawn' and start again. Such multi-branched stories pitched at the right language level are highly motivating for usually reluctant readers. My own experience has been that writing second person narratives, especially if broken down into scene-by-scene fragments, can often generate the same degree of enthusiasm.

Third person

The third person perspective is familiar to most pupils even before they are formally introduced to it. It is the most common way of framing a narrative and the only point I feel that needs to be made here is to be aware of what I call full third person and partial third person. In the former case the reader's point of attention actually does move from place to place and character to character, mirroring what the author has done in creating the work. Partial third person still uses the 'he-she voice' but the focus stays with one character throughout. A professional author will intend this of course, but when it appears in a pupil's writing it can indicate a failure to visualize beyond that single character. The young writer might not have an overview of 'the wider world of the story' and there is little if any exploration beyond the focus-character's immediate circumstances. I have called this 'parrot-on-the-shoulder-itis' because the reader is trapped like a parrot sitting on the focus-character's shoulder throughout the story. In a full third person narrative the parrot flies from place to place with ease.

Module 6

Person

First, second and third person

The idea of *person* when we write is whether we are speaking to ourselves (what I call the 'I-voice'), directly to someone else (the 'you-voice') or about somebody (the 'he or she-voice'). These ways of speaking are known as the first person, second person and third person. Another way of understanding it is like this:

▶ As an author when I write something I am the *first person* to know about it.

▶ When I tell you, you are the *second person* to find out.

▶ If we then went and told Joe Bloggs he'd be the *third person* to hear the news.

Examples of first, second and third person writing

This is what these ways of speaking look like in practice:

First person: *I'm walking down a long dark passageway in the Haunted Mansion. I feel very nervous because I can hear strange sounds coming from the floor above. I reach a flight of stairs and can either climb them to investigate or pass them by and continue along the corridor. I don't know what to do!*

Notice also how I've written this as though it were happening now, in the present. This is called the *present tense*. Of course I could also write this scene as though it had happened in the past (past tense) or could happen in the future (future tense). But let's get back to the notion of person.

If I wrote my scene in the second person it would look like this:

Second person: *You're walking down a long dark passageway in the Haunted Mansion. You feel very nervous because you can hear strange sounds coming from the floor above. You reach a flight of stairs and can either climb them to investigate or pass them by and continue along the corridor. You don't know what to do!*

Notice how this is written in the present tense. If you've ever read a 'choose your own adventure' book you'll have noticed that they are written in the second person. It's as though you (the reader) were a character in the story. These modules are also in the second person because I'm speaking directly to you about these ideas.

The third person is perhaps the most common way of writing. You'll recognise it at once. Here's our scene written that way – note that if your character was female you'd simply change 'he' to 'she' and 'him' to 'her':

> *He was walking down a long dark passageway in the Haunted Mansion. He felt very nervous because he could hear strange sounds coming from the floor above. He reached a flight of stairs and could either climb them to investigate or pass them by and continue along the corridor. He didn't know what to do!*

Notice how this scene is also in the past tense, which is the way third person writing usually looks. When we talk about the person and tense of a piece of writing we are speaking generally. Look at this:

> *Later when Steve had escaped from the mansion he went round to his friend Ben's house and told him all about it. 'I was walking down a long dark passageway,' he said 'and felt very nervous because I could hear strange sounds coming from the floor above.'*

The story as a whole is being told in the third person, but what Steve says is written in the first person because he is talking about himself at this point. But there's no need to get technical about this. What's important to realise is that:

► When you write in the first person you get right inside your character and can tell the reader about his (or her) thoughts and feelings second by second. The disadvantage about it is that you, and therefore the reader, have to stay with that character all through the story.

► Writing in the second person (and present tense) puts the reader right there in the action. The reader *is* the character. That can make the experience of the story very exciting and 'immediate'. The disadvantage is that, a bit like first person, you are stuck with one character's viewpoint – unless you wanted to experiment and write different scenes or chapters from different characters' perspectives. There's nothing stopping you of course, but you must make sure the reader knows very clearly whose eyes (s)he's looking through!

► Writing in the third person gives you the advantage of being able to leap about in space, from character to character. Simply by saying 'Meanwhile across the Atlantic Ben was recruiting his team of haunted house investigators' you can have leaped thousands of miles and into Ben's life in a single sentence. That's why most stories are written this way.

The choice is yours of course. In fact, you probably decided which person to use much earlier in your planning. If so, when you think about your next story consider switching person just for a change.

Module 6

Impersonal writing

Note: There is another way of writing called 'impersonal' because it doesn't refer to me or you or him or her. This is what it looks like . . .

Haunted mansions often contain long dark passageways that can easily cause nervousness, especially if strange sounds are heard from the floor above. It would be difficult to decide whether to climb a flight of stairs to investigate or simply pass them by and continue along the corridor.

This kind of style is more usually suited to non-fiction writing and is not often found in stories.

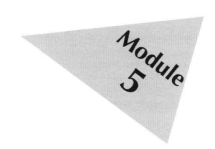

Style

Helping pupils to find a style

Style is one of those wonderfully intangible aspects of writing that is difficult to analyse and almost impossible to measure, although we know when it's there and realise that it's a powerful influence on our appreciation of the work. I think of written style as I think of the individuality of someone's voice. I can make comments about pitch, timbre, volume, pace, tone and content – but what is it about the way these things work together that make a voice so charismatic that I could listen to it all day, or so unbearably irritating that I want to shut it off at once? Similarly, with the style of any author's writing. What is it that gives those words their distinctiveness? Certainly the reader's personal opinion plays a part. I remember recommending one of my favourite authors to a friend, pointing out that the writer's style moved me often and sometimes to tears, during the course of a novel. A week later my friend gave the book back and told me she found it trite, flat and uninteresting. 'But what about the sense of wonder his language evokes? That sense of nostalgic longing for things gone by, and yet the incredible optimism for the future? What about the *style*!' My friend looked at me tolerantly. 'What style?' she wanted to know. Such is the elusive quality of what I'm trying to define.

Inspiring confidence

Having said that I think every effort should be made to encourage pupils to recognise and feel confident to talk about the many and varied aspects of an author's style. How do we know that a story was written by that particular author? Beyond the themes, genre and sequence of events comprising the work, what made it a pleasure (or not) to read? We can take an analytical approach and talk about the degree of formality, intended audience, choice of vocabulary, use of first or third person and so on, but that helps only to a certain point. Then the world, as the philosopher Alan Watts so playfully noted, becomes 'fuzzy'. It's like trying to describe chocolate to someone who's never tasted it. Watts' advice of course would be simply to give that person a piece of chocolate so they could taste it for themselves! Perhaps ultimately an author's style is the whole that's more than the sum of the parts, in which case we're back to organics. Style is a quality which, I feel, evolves through the experience of writing. After penning (or these days keying) a million words, an aspiring author's style is more in evidence. Most of the

Module 5

pupils we teach won't get that far or would want to, but we can support any efforts they make in walking along that very personal road of indeterminate length and infinite variety:

▶ By realising that in the end the secret of good writing cannot be analysed out. To try and do so is what the Japanese call 'slitting the throat of the skylark to see what makes it sing'. Style is a synthesis of everything a writer does. We can teach pupils to appreciate it and encourage them to value it in their own work and, through a playful enjoyment of making meanings out of words, to develop it within them.

▶ Many teachers I've met seem to want a quick fix in helping the pupils to produce 'quality writing'. Alas all too often this seems to be whatever gets pupils through the SATs. It is an eternal dilemma in education generally. Learning can't be forced. If it is then the result is not understanding and a love of knowledge but at worst anxiety, insecurity and apathy. Even pupils who succeed in the system by attaining high scores and gaining paper qualifications may not be inspired to take their learning beyond school. Ironically when pupils feel relaxed and self-assured and are enjoying what they do then their capability (and ultimately their test results) will increase. But why am I telling you this? You know it already.

▶ Value it before you evaluate. For some pupils even minimal and 'low quality' writing is a great achievement. Once we recognise that and praise it sincerely then the pupils recognise it too and have something substantial to build on. Recently I ran a workshop in which many of the young writers seemed to enjoy the work. Some were confident enough to read it out and did so with pleasure. Their teacher's comment was typically 'Well I was looking for something more imaginative,' and in one case 'Oh no, not zombies again!' Even if that's your reaction, what educational value resides in telling the pupil so?

▶ Enthusiasm communicates. When you are enthusiastic about words and writing your energy radiates out to the pupils. When they write, write with them and walk the road as a fellow traveller. The origin of the word 'enthusiasm' incidentally is the Greek *en* + *theos*, to be inspired (inspirited) by God. The spirit of the work is the song of the skylark and that can never be reduced to data.

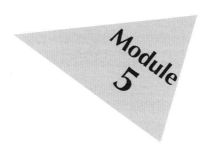

Style

The bigger picture

Talking of 'style', what on Earth does that mean? Generally it's the manner or the sort of writing you do – except that those words don't really sum it up. Think about what we mean when we say that a person has style. That would include her appearance, way of talking, the kind of person she would like us to think she is. In fact a person's style is a blend of many different characteristics. It's the whole bundle, the big picture.

Writing style is the same kind of thing. As you've worked through this book you have made many different decisions about what your story will be like. When you write it what comes out will reflect the choices you've made. But more than that, you'll be trying to tell that story *in your own particular way* – and that's the best way to do it of course. The more you strive to be yourself in the way you write, the more you will be developing your own individual style.

Taking your time

Much of this book has been about quick and hopefully useful ways of having ideas, plus tips and techniques for actually writing them down. Style however is not something that's instant; it develops over time, through your experience of writing many, many stories. There's no short cut to style.

So why am I bothering to tell you about it? Well as a way of encouraging you to keep writing for a start. Being able to use language clearly and powerfully is a valuable tool in life. Words influence people every day in all sorts of ways. But more than that, using words well is a great pleasure, whether you turn them into stories, poems, essays, letters, diaries, emails or whatever. Some people, like myself, enjoy it so much that we've made it a way of life. Most of you perhaps won't want to take it that far, but whatever effort you put into expressing your thoughts in words will bring you rewards and will take you closer to having your own personal style of using language.

Strong start and finish

Useful classroom tips

We all know the good sense of this so I feel there is no need to elaborate on the idea or argue the case. How can we help to ensure that the pupils achieve it? Here are some tips:

► Once the pupils have a basic storyline in mind get them to think about the end of the story first. What are the components of memorable endings in books and films? – not the details of setting and character but the emotional qualities; the drama, excitement, shock, humour and so on.

► Help the pupils write brief 'recipe cards' of the ingredients of strong endings. Take a good handful of danger, add some time-running-out and mix with a little frustration that the villain is escaping . . . And so on.

► Show young writers how to 'hit the ground running' when they open a story. It doesn't have to be an all-action scene: atmosphere can be established quickly, a mystery introduced, a hint of danger suggested. What will make the reader want to read on? Get the pupils to learn by example. Show them ten great opening scenes. Tease out the common elements. Set pupils the assignment of just writing an opening based on what they've learned. They can finish the story later (and may well be more motivated to do so when they return refreshed to the task). Boost pupils' enthusiasm for finishing a story strongly by giving them time and the strategies to plan out the whole story well. Young writers often falter and give up because they 'run out of ideas'. That issue can be dealt with much earlier in the thinking and planning stages.

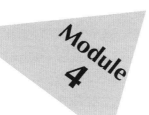

Strong start and finish

A good opening

Here are a few opening sentences that I think are good:

► The knife flashed down. There was a brief scream, then silence.

► They had only met a week ago, yet even as she kissed him she knew it would be for the last time.

► Something moved ahead in the shadows. Two small burning red lights appeared – the creature's eyes. They were fifteen feet above the ground.

► Steve was halfway down the street when he realised that he still had his slippers on – and then to his horror noticed he was wearing his dressing gown not his overcoat.

The first opener presents us with an immediate shock. There's no buildup, we're straight into the story. In the second we wonder at the events behind the girl thinking she won't be kissing her new boyfriend again. The third story starter presents us with a mystery – what is the huge creature? And it's a bit unnerving that it should be so close. In the fourth opener we have a mystery too; why is Steve walking about in slippers and dressing gown? And there's a little humour in there too.

Useful tips

The whole point of a strong start to your story is to make the reader want to carry on reading. So a good opener is one that delivers a fast emotional punch (a shock, a shiver, a laugh), raises a question or mystery, or at least drops the reader into the middle of some action. If you are writing a short story (as opposed to something much longer) it's important to get on with the plot: don't hold things up with long explanations or descriptions. Just jump in and get going.

► If you haven't actually written your story yet, bear these points in mind as you start to write. If you have written it, look back and check your story start in your *Review*.

▶ Look at the opening scenes of short stories you've enjoyed. What have the authors done to catch your interest straight away? (If you think an author hasn't achieved that, what was in the story that interested or impressed you?)

A good ending

Story endings also need to be strong and memorable. In the world of acting there is a saying – 'Leave them wanting more.' And I think that's good advice for stories too. You probably already know that the last part of the story is called the resolution. This is usually where the hero solves the main problem created by the villain (see **Basic narrative elements (Module 42)**). The villain is justly punished, the hero is rewarded in some way and life gets back to normal. I say 'usually', but you can break that rule if you want to. In the tale I mentioned earlier (see **Timespans (Module 12)**), Andros wakes up and is immediately killed by the man-rat. End of story. My hope was that the shock ending would make my readers want to go on to the next story in the collection.

Story endings must satisfy in a different way to story starters. As a writer you need to have tied up any loose ends in the plot, dealt with any unanswered questions and generally 'rounded things off'. Notice that in the Andros story, although he gets killed, readers know what Mankind's fate has been. There's no sense of 'Yes, but what happened?' All has been made clear, and that's the satisfaction I'm talking about. Like eating a well-prepared meal, you feel satisfied but can still say 'Oo, I could eat that again!' It's the same with well-told stories.

▶ Think back to stories you've enjoyed. Did the authors leave you wanting more? What did the stories contain to achieve that?

▶ Some authors start their stories without knowing how they will end. In this case the resolution unfolds in the writing. That's one way of doing it. If you decide to write that way, bear in mind what a good ending should contain even if you don't yet know the details.

▶ Only leave loose ends and unanswered questions if you intend to write a sequel. Even then the story must satisfy the reader and not leave them puzzled.

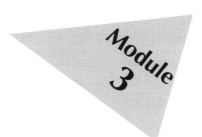

Presentation

Making work public

Essentially the meaning of 'publish' is 'to make public' and that's the rationale I use as I encourage pupils to be neat and accurate in their work. A person's writing represents them to the world. The way it looks as much as what it says creates an impression – and while it is true that one should never judge a book by its cover, an author is inevitably judged by her writing.

When I urge pupils to take care over the presentation of their work I tell them it's like getting ready to go out somewhere – you take some time and effort to look presentable. So should it be with final-draft stories. I also like to recount an anecdote about my late father-in-law who was an industrial chemist in charge of a big R&D lab with a sizeable budget. Whenever a job vacancy came up Des would invariably receive scores of applications, many of them from people with a Master's or even Ph.D. His instruction to his secretary was to 'Bin the letters that have not been addressed neatly and clearly without even opening them. Open the ones that remain and merely glance at the applications. Discard the ones that are untidy, badly punctuated and with words misspelled. Then filter what remains according to the company's standard guidelines and give me the few that are left.' On one occasion Des's secretary made the point that some of the discarded applicants might be just perfect for the job. 'That's true,' came the reply, 'but the job involves expensive and dangerous chemicals and if people aren't bothered about attending to the small details in their letters, they may well not attend to them in their work.'

Early on in an author's career, if an editor or reader receives a poorly presented manuscript then she might not trouble to read past the first few pages. Apart from that, published authors too have to present their work as neatly, accurately and clearly as they can, as well as taking account of the specific guidelines of publishers' 'house styles'. Ignoring these is not looked upon favourably.

Having said all that, working under test conditions again throws up the dilemma of writing creatively while bearing neatness and accuracy in mind given time constraints. It will always be a compromise especially for those pupils whose handwriting deteriorates when it is rushed. I don't think there's an answer to this unless or until coursework forms part of the assessment together with ongoing teacher evaluation.

(Please note there are no **Teacher's notes** for **Modules 17–15**.)

Module 3

Presentation

Getting presentation right

I have a confession to make. My handwriting is terrible. I remember once when I was aged ten my teacher put a big red line through a story I'd written and told me to 'Do it again!' That nearly put me off writing for life. He also said once that my handwriting looked as though a spider had run through a puddle of ink and then scurried across my page. I thought that was quite funny, though of course I didn't dare laugh out loud.

Notice that we're talking about handwriting here, not writing in the sense of *composing* the story. Lots of authors, even very famous ones, have untidy handwriting. Did that stop them? No way. Getting the story down on paper is the most important thing. They know they can tidy up later.

Planning your time

Young writers in school have this particular problem, especially in tests, where you are judged on the neatness of your handwriting even though you may have been told to write quickly because you have limited time. That doesn't seem fair to me, but I don't suppose the situation will change in the short term. The answer here is to plan your story so that you can pay some attention to doing your neatest handwriting and have time to go back at the end to check spellings and punctuation.

Why presentation is important

OK, maybe you're thinking 'Oh no, he goes on about it just like my teacher does!' Well that's because both your teacher and I think that the presentation of your work is important. Your work says something about you. It *represents* you. Do you feel pleased to have completed your story? Do you take pride in it? Do you have that sense of self-respect which is so important to a person's confidence? If you do then I don't need to convince you any more. If not, then perhaps you'll think about this:

▶ Never let untidy handwriting or poor spelling and punctuation stop you from telling your story. You are still learning, and any reasonable adult will appreciate this.

Module 3

▶ Accurate spelling and punctuation make what you want to say clearer. Under normal circumstances you can check these in your Review time. Under test conditions what's most important is to stay calm and focused as you write. If you're not sure of a spelling, no need to panic. Just write what you think is the correct way and move on. Same with punctuation. Put what you think is right and move on.

▶ Always strive to do your best and never mind what other people are doing. Something else that I think is unfair is the way that young writers in schools are judged in comparison to each other, or according to someone's belief about what the 'average ten-year-old' should be able to do. Have you ever met an average ten-year-old? I haven't. Every one I've met (and that goes for kids of other ages too) is unique and individual. But hey, that's just me grumbling. When you know you've done your best you can take pride in yourself. When my school friend Anthony Morris got higher grades than me for stories I felt upset, but really I shouldn't have. And what's most important is that I never stopped writing and trying to improve.

Module 2

A writer's responsibilities

Your obligations as a writer

Near the start of this Countdown you read about a Writer's Rights (Module 57). But you know that with rights come responsibilities. I'm using that word to mean 'duties and obligations'; things you must do out of a sense of honour and pride and respect – not just because someone has told you to do them. Different people may have other ideas about a writer's obligations, but this is what I think:

▶ Your first duty is to yourself, to do the best you can in your writing. That's about *self*-respect, which I think is vital before you can truly and fully respect other people.

▶ If you intend for other people to look at your work, then you have a responsibility to them also. You can honour such an obligation mainly by having done your best. But take time to check that your work is presented as neatly and clearly as you can. This helps to give your reader the best possible experience the story can deliver.

▶ I believe it's always easier to criticise than to create. If people criticise your work it's worth wondering if *they* ever sit down to write. When you receive a criticism, separate the bad feelings you might have from any possible good advice the critic intends. That person may have done you a favour by showing you a way to improve. And because you know what it feels like to be criticised, use those feelings to become more tolerant of other people's work. Making someone else feel small just makes you smaller too.

▶ A most brilliant Japanese poet, a man called Matsuo Basho, once said 'Learn the rules well and then forget them.' In other words just get on and enjoy the experience of writing. Remember you are still learning 'the rules' and the best way to master them is to have fun in your work.

In the mood for writing

Being in the mood

There's a cynical saying which goes 'When all's said and done, there's more said than done.' Well I've said a lot in this book and you've been very patient reading through it. I hope it's helped. And now it's time for me to get on with another story and time for you to launch into your story and fly.

Some useful tips

But what if you don't feel in the mood? What if, after all the advice I've given and the preparations you've made, you simply don't feel like sitting down to write? That happens to me sometimes (though not often these days) and I've found the following things help:

▶ If I'm feeling upset and angry, first, I try and sort out the problem that's troubling me. If I can't do that, I write in my diary. I rant and rave and swear and let all the feelings come out on paper. Afterwards, I feel a lot better and can usually get on with my life and my story.

▶ I try to arrange my conditions so that they make writing more comfortable. Your writing environment is important. Are you physically comfortable? Do you have enough light and fresh air? Have you cut down on distractions as much as you can? Sometimes of course it's difficult or impossible to arrange for the perfect environment, but do what's possible to make the physical task of writing easier.

▶ I'm lucky enough to have a little spot in my house where I write (no, not the cupboard under the stairs!). I go to that place each time and just by sitting down at my desk and picking up my story stone the words start to come. It's like a switch in my brain flicking on.

A story stone?

Oh, are you wondering what a story stone is? It's a pebble, just an ordinary pebble I found once on the beach. I used it first as a paperweight, but when I was writing

I realised that if the words wouldn't flow and I felt stuck, I'd pick up the pebble and holding it would kind of relax me, and then I knew how to carry on. After that whenever I felt good about a scene I'd written, and especially when I had that lovely glow upon finishing a story, I'd deliberately hold the pebble and link it with all the good feelings.

What I was doing (though I didn't understand it at the time) was to create a link in my brain with being able to write well and the feel of that pebble in my hand. The story stone said to my brain cells, 'OK, remember what it's like when the ideas and words are flowing. Do that again now.' And my brain did!

A story stone is an incredibly useful piece of kit. Ask your teacher more about this idea.

► Finally, the writing itself shows you best how to move on and improve. Every word you write is another step along the road to getting better. Even when you've struggled and sweated over your work (as every writer has) remember that you are pointed in that brilliant direction – onwards and upwards . . .

And now – hey – what's that great feeling building up inside? No, it's not wind, it's . . .

BLASTOFF!

Review

So here we are. You have a story that you've written in front of you. Are you pleased with it? Are you at least just a little bit proud? You should be, because to have done all that thinking and then put it into words is a real achievement. Well done.

If you are anything like me you probably have other story ideas that you want to tackle. At the same time, maybe there's a little voice in your mind telling you to check what you've already just done, to be sure it's the best it can be. Listen to that voice, because it belongs to the pride and the pleasure that you are enjoying.

Two questions

When I look back at work I've done I ask myself two questions:

1   Is there anything I can change to make this story the best I can do today?
2   What have I learned in writing this that will make my next story even better?

If I thought about my story before I wrote it, and if I chose my words carefully and carried on thinking *as* I wrote it, then there's probably not too much more that I need to do to it. You have probably done some work in school about *drafting*. A draft is a 'rough copy' of a document. The idea behind this is that what comes out first time is nowhere near complete and that there's still a lot more thinking to do about it (the story in our case).

Well that may be true *but not necessarily*. Some authors have a rough idea for their story and just start to write to see what ideas appear. That draft is a rough copy, with all kinds of things that need to be deleted, changed, extended and so on. When this happens then a redraft is needed. This might be a total rewrite that includes all the new thinking.

On the other hand, sometimes a story comes out and it's almost exactly what the author wants it to be, apart perhaps from a few little things that need to be altered. In that case there's no need to write it all out again: the structure of the story is sound and only some details need to be changed. No redraft is needed, just 'polishing up' what's already there. One advantage of writing on a computer of course is that these changes can be done quickly and without much effort, which is why I recommend you do that whenever you can.

Some people who are involved in education think that redrafting work must always be part of the process. But I disagree. If a 'first draft' story works, leave it alone (apart from the little changes mentioned above). I also think it's strange that pupils are told to draft and redraft – and yet when the exams come along they're not given time to do that. I wonder why?

Anyway, what's important is that you feel you've done your best. Will your story be perfect? Of course not. Will everybody love it? Of course not. That's not the point. You dared to do it and you did your best, and that's what counts.

Look back at the second review question. It's important, because it means that *you can learn useful things even from the mistakes you make*. Also, it means that you are not sitting around waiting to be told how you can improve your writing – you are actively searching for answers yourself. That is a powerful thing to do and something that your teachers are likely to be very pleased about.

Feeling pleased with your achievement, actively looking to improve, getting excited about your next story . . . These are the things that turn you from a writer into an author.

What do I mean by that? Well add the letters 'ity' to author and you get – no, not 'ityauthor' – but authority. An authority is someone who has influence, who will not get pushed around. An authority will listen to advice but makes up her (or his) own mind. An authority at best is independent yet flexible, sets high standards but remains tolerant, has a mature outlook but a childlike heart. Apply that to the writing you do and you are an author.

Well that's about it. You've counted down with me through some important stages of thinking about a story. And what has come out of it? Not just a bunch of words on a page but, as the author Ezra Pound has said, 'a ball of light in your hands'. Thinking about a story in that way shows you can shine, and it lights the way for your next adventure.

Bibliography

Booker, Christopher (2004) *The Seven Basic Plots: why we tell stories*. London: Continuum. This is an extensive exploration of the seven archetypal themes that inform human experience and story.

Bowkett, Stephen (2001) *ALPS StoryMaker: using fiction as a resource for accelerated learning*. Stafford and London: Network Educational Press/Network Continuum.

Bowkett, Stephen (2003) *StoryMaker Catch Pack: using genre fiction as a resource for accelerated learning*. Stafford: Network Educational Press.

Bowkett, Stephen (2007) *100+ Ideas for Teaching Creativity*. London: Continuum.

Bowkett, Stephen (2007) *Jumpstart! Creativity*. London and New York: David Fulton (Routledge).

Bowkett, Stephen (2007) *A Handbook of Creative Learning Activities*. London: Network Continuum.

Bowkett, S. *et al.* (2007) *Success in the Creative Classroom: using past wisdom to inspire excellence*. London: Network Continuum.

Ekwall, Eilert (1981) *The Concise Oxford Dictionary of Place Names*. Oxford: Clarendon Press (OUP).

Gardner, Howard (1993) *Multiple Intelligences in Theory and Practice*. New York: Basic Books.

Law, Stephen (2002) *The Philosophy Files*. London: Orion.

Owen, Nick (2001) *The Magic of Metaphor*. Bancyfelin: Crown House.

Propp, V. (2001) *Morphology of the Folktale*. Austin, TX: University of Texas Press.

Rocket, M. and Percival, S. (2002) *Thinking for Learning*. Stafford: Network Educational Press.

Rowland, M. (2005) *The Philosopher at the End of the Universe*. London: Ebury Press.

Smith, Manuel J. (1975) *When I Say No, I Feel Guilty*. New York: Bantam (Doubleday).

Stanley, Sara and Bowkett, Stephen (2004) *But Why? Developing philosophical thinking in the classroom*. Stafford: Network Educational Press.

Thomas, Dylan (1994) *The Followers*. London: J.M. Dent.

Tilling, Mike (2001) *Adventures in Learning*. Stafford: Network Educational Press. This book explores the relationship between narrative structures and the personal 'stories' of individual learners in terms of the useful metaphor of the 'learning journey'.

Voytilla, S. (1999) *Myth and the Movies: discovering the mythic structure of 50 unforgettable films*. Studio City, CA: Michael Weise Productions.

Wallas, Lee (1985) *Stories for the Third Ear*. New York: Norton.

Williams, Pat (1998) *How Stories Heal*. Chalvington, Sussex: European Therapy Studies Institute.

Index

(Numbers refer to Module numbers. **Bold** numbers indicate that the topic appears in the **Teacher's notes**.)

Gardner, H. *see* linguistic intelligence
genre as distinct from 'form' **46**, **37**, 37

handwriting 3
Hill, Douglas, children's author **40**

if-then game for exploring causes, effect and consequence **54**
if-then-because game for exploring character **24**
'imitate, innovate, tnvent' (from Pie Corbett) 37
inspiration **51**
INSPIRED acronym 51
interview game for characters 24

libel 27
linguistic intelligence **48**; and literacy **29**, **21**

matchbox characters 24
Maugham, Somerset and three golden rules for writing – *Overview*
'meanwhile game' and connectives **7**
metacognition **55**
metaphors **49**; and similes 8
minimal writing as a strategy for motivation and planning **40**
minisagas, 50-word stories for editing and economy of language **9**
modelling the process of writing **60**
morality, philosophical discussion and Crime stories **33**
motifs **41**

narrative elements **42**
narrative, etymology of 56
narrative intelligence **48**
narrative lines **38**

'organic' processes in writing – *Overview*, **21**
originality **54**
'overwhelm' as an inhibitor of creativity **55**, **9–4**

personification **31**
photo story 10
pie chart for characters 24
planning **40**
play format 44
playfulness **59**
pole-bridging as 'muttering your understanding' **48**, **38**
prequel **30**
principles for developing creativity **57**
publish as in 'making public' 29

questioning and the creative process **59**, 59
questions open and closed 24

redrafting and economy of language **9**
research 21
resolution 4
rights 57
ritual and creativity **58**

SATs **57**
'show don't tell' **50**, **34**
signs *see* abstract art
Six Big Important Questions 52, **39**; and the writing environment 39
story boarding 10
story, etymology of 56
story 'recipes' 33
story stone as an anchoring technique 1